透明水彩で描く

INTRODUCTION TO

WATERCOLOR

PAINTING

INTRODUCTION TO
WATERCOLOR PAINTING

Copyright © 1991 by Graphic-sha Publishing Co., Ltd.
1-9-12, Kudan-kita, Chiyoda-ku Tokyo 102. Japan

ISBN4-7661-0622-9

Printed in Japan
First Printing, Mar. 1991

透明水彩で描く・目次

WATERECOLOR PAINTING CONTENTS

翻訳　Gavin Frew
レイアウト　株式会社エイジ

はじめに
Foreword

　透明水彩の魅力は"新鮮で軽やかな色彩がかもしだす透明感"にあります。その魅力は，絵具と水と紙，そして筆さばきから生まれるのです。透明水彩の技法はやさしいものから高度なものまでありますが，いくつかの基本をマスターすれば，あとはその応用です。本書は基本に始まり，即実践に役立つよういろいろな対象を描くコツを図解と実例で示しております。また，実例とともに失敗しがちな例を付け加え，初心者に役立つようにしました。

The beauty of transparent watercolors lies in 'the translucent feel of the fresh, bright colors' and this beauty is the result of a combination of paint, paper and brushstrokes. The techniques utilized in water-color painting range from the simple to the very advanced but once one has mastered a few of the basics, one is ready to start putting them into practice. This book starts with the basic techniques uses a series of examples and explanatory diagrams to show how they can be used to paint a wide variety of subjects. It also shows examples of common mistakes in watercolor painting and is designed to be of use to all beginners.

1 章
画材と用具の使い方

Chapter 1
Using the Paints and Equipment

上達のためのアドバイス
Advice on How to Advance

用紙と筆の選択を誤るな

　良い透明水彩を描くには，1に用紙，2に筆，3に技術といってもよい。なぜなら，良い用紙や筆は，技術を補ってくれる力があるからで，筆や用紙を無頓着に選ぶと，使いこなすことが難しくなるからである。技術は繰り返しを積み重ねるとカバーできるのは確かではあるが，筆や用紙の選択を誤ると技術を身につけるまで時間のロスも多く無駄になってしまう。

はっきりした線で下描きする

　下描きが薄いと，最初の明るい色を塗っただけで見えなくなって，次の色をスムーズにあつかえなくなってしまう。白い用紙の上の線はかなり濃く見えるが，色を塗ると気にならないものだ。鉛筆はBがちょうどよいが，陰影の調子は透明水彩ほんらいの発色を損なってしまうので，線描にすること。

彩色は明るい色から始める

　最初に彩色する色は，太めの筆にたっぷり含ませ，下描きの輪郭線からはみ出すぐらいに大胆に塗ろう。明るい色から彩色すれば，はみ出しても次に塗る色でカバーできるから心配無用だ。したがって，最初の明るい色は，できるだけ広範囲に塗っておくとよい。ただし，黄色と紫，赤と緑のように補色同士は混ざるとグレーになるので重ねることは避けること。

Don't make a mistake in choosing paper and brushes

It is true to say that the most important things in watercolor painting are first the paper, second the brushes and third technique, the reason being that the correct paper and brushes make painting much easier. If the paper or brushes are chosen without care, it makes it difficult to master the techniques and although it is not impossible with practice, the time spent trying to master the wrong equipment could be better spent learning more advanced techniques.

Draw the rough sketch clearly

If the lines of the sketch are too light, they will be hidden by the first coat of paint and this will make adding the second coat much harder. Although the lines may stand out awfully on the white paper, when they have had some paint applied over them, they do not notice at all. A 'B' grade of pencil is ideal, but do not add any shading to the sketch as it will show through the paint and detract from its luminosity, just draw the outline.

Start with the lightest colors

Add the first color using a large brush with plenty of paint on it. Do not worry if the paint goes beyond the lines of the sketch as you will be painting the light colors first and they will be hidden when you add the later colors. Paint the first light color over as large an area as possible but try not to use opposite colors like yellow and violet or red and green over each other (complimentary colors mix to produce grey).

濃くはっきりした線で下描きすること。
色が重なると線は気にならない。
下描きの線が薄いと，最初の彩色段階で
迷ってしまう。

Draw the sketch with firm, dark lines. The lines
will not stand out once they have been painted
over. If the sketch is too light, it will be confusing
later when painting.

最初彩色の明るい色は，できるだけ広く
塗る。輪郭線からはみだしても構わない。
部分的に彩色すると色が散らばって見え
るので，まとめにくい。

The first color should be the lightest color. Paint it
as widely as possible and do not worry if you cross
the lines of the sketch. If the color is added in
small sections the picture will appear broken up
and lack continuity.

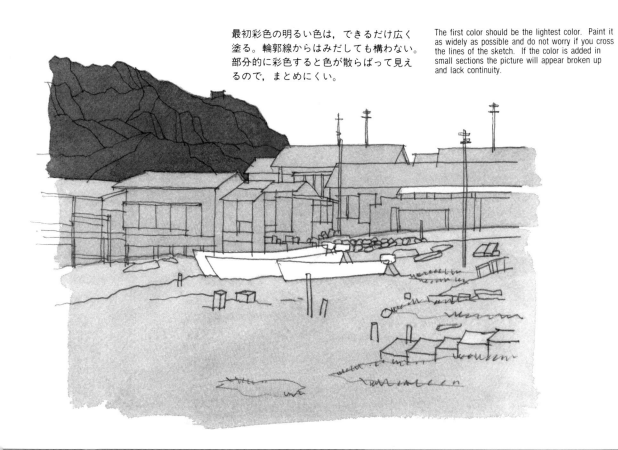

透明水彩思考で描く
Transparent Watercolors Should be Used Thoughtfully

　透明水彩は，最初に明るい色を塗り，次第に暗い色を塗り重ねて完成させる彩色手順を基本としている。この彩色手順で大切なのは"暗い部分を塗りながら，明るい部分を描く"という透明水彩ならではの思考をもつことである。

　思考というと難しいと思うだろうが，実際に試してみると意外にやさしい。

　簡単にいえば，最初に塗った明るい色の部分の形は，次の色を重ねて仕上げる技法である。

　右ページの家と草の図をご覧いただこう。まず草の部分を塗る。次に家を塗りながら草の形を仕上げる。つまり草と家が同時進行で描かれていることがお分かりになるだろう。

　透明水彩的思考とは，明るい色から塗り始めるという彩色手順を踏まえたうえで，1つのタッチを隣合う2つの要素と関連づけていくことにある。

The basic technique when using transparent watercolors is to paint the lighter colors first then gradually add the darker ones. When using this technique, it is important to bear in mind that 'you will be depicting the lighter areas as you paint the darker areas.' This may sound rather difficult to understand, but in practice, it is not. To put it a bit more simply it is this, the shape that you paint first with light colors will be improved upon as you add the darker ones.
Let us look at the picture of the house on the right hand page. First the area of grass is filled in then the details are added to the grass as the house is painted. In other words, the grass is painted at the same time as the house.
It is important to remember when painting in transparent watercolors not only do you start with light colors and then progress through the darker ones, but also, each stroke of the brush will affect the areas to either side.

最初に明るい草を塗る。建物の暗い色を重ねて草の形を描くので，実際の色面より大きくはみだして塗っておく。

First paint the light color of the grass. The details will be added when painting the dark color of the house, so the green should overlap the house area.

建物の暗い色を塗りながら，草の形を描き起こしていく。透明色は，暗い色を塗ってから明るい色で描き起こすことはできない。

Paint in the shape of the grass while adding the dark color of the house. With transparent colors, it is impossible to add a light color after a dark one has been painted.

絵具とパレット
Paint and the Palette

絵具 チューブ入りの透明水彩用の絵具は，パレットに詰めて完全に乾燥させたものを彩色用としている。基本色としては，筆者のパレットにある24色を示したので参考にしていただきたい。画材メーカーによって色名の頭にパーマネントとかカドミウム，あるいはネオという言葉をつけているが，これの有無はあまり関係ない。購入するときは，イエローならイエローライトかイエローディープかをはっきり指定するとよろしい。

パレット 2つに折れるもの，金属製，プラスティック製などいろいろあるが，写真のように仕切りの多いタイプが便利。

Paint : Tube watercolor paints should be put on the palette and allowed to completely dry before use. To give some idea of the basic colors, the twenty-four colors on the author's palette are as listed.

Manufacturers of watercolor paints often precede the name of a color with the words 'permanent,' 'cadmium' or 'neo,' but these do not make any difference to the artist. When buying paints what is important is to make sure that you get either a light color or deep color as necessary.

Palette : There are many kinds of palette, ones that can be folded into two, ones that are made of metal and those that are made of plastic, however, a palette with a large number of sections, like the one shown in the photograph, is very useful.

①レモンイエロー
Lemon Yellow

②カドミウムイエロー
ディープ
Cadmium Yellow Deep

③カドミウムオレンジ
Cadmium Orange

④カドミウムレッド
ディープ
Cadmium Red Deep

⑤パーマネントローズ
Permanent Rose

⑥クリムソンレーキ
Crimson Lake

⑦マゼンタ
Magenta

⑧パーマネント
バイオレット
Permanent Violet

⑨ウルトラマリンライト
Ultramarine Light

⑩セルリアンブルー
Cerulean Blue

⑪プルッシアンブルー

Prussian Blue

⑯パーマネントグリーン No 1

Permanent Green No.1

㉑ネープルスイエロー

Naples Yellow

⑫ペイニーズグレー

Payne's Grey

⑰オリーブグリーン

Olive Green

㉒イエローオーカー

Yellow Ochre

⑬エメラルドグリーン

Emerald Green

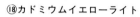

⑱カドミウムイエローライト

Cadmium Yellow Light

㉓バーントシェンナー

Burnt Sienna

⑭ウインザーグリーン

Windsor Green

⑲バーミリオン

Vermilion

㉔セピア

Sepia

⑮パーマネントグリーン No 2

Permanent Green No.2

⑳カドミウムレッドディープ

Cadmium Red Deep

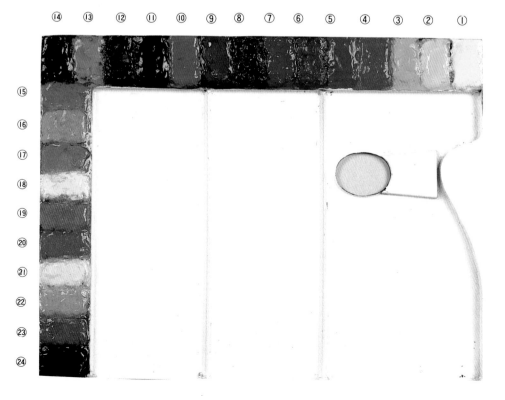

絵具を溶く
Using the Paint

　チューブ入りの絵具は，仕切りいっぱい平らに詰めて固めて使う。1度に詰めると中のほうがなかなか固まらないので，1週間に3分の1を出して，3週間位で詰め終わるようにするとよい。

　色は絵具を溶く水加減で，薄く（明るい）も濃くもなる。基本的な彩色は，筆にたっぷり含ませて行うので，多めに溶いておくとよい。

Fill each section of the palette with paint and allow it to dry before use. If the section is filled in one step, the paint will take a long time to dry so it is best if the section is filled one third at a time over a period of about three weeks.
The shade of the paint used changes with the amount of water on the brush. As a general rule, one should fill the brush with paint when painting so it is best if a lot of paint is dissolved when using.

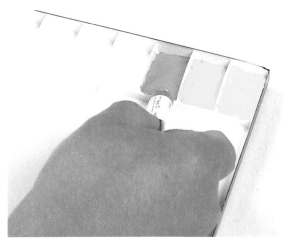

チューブ入りの絵具はパレットに出して，固めたものを彩色に使う。

Tube paint that has been allowed to dry on the palette is used for coloring.

1

絵具の溶き方
1，水を含ませた筆をパレットのへりでしごいて水を切る。
2，固めてある絵具を筆に含ませる。
3，パレットに残った水で溶いてから彩色する。

How to Dissolve the Paint.
1. Fill the brush with water then squeeze off the excess on the edge of the palette.
2. Soak the paint with the brush.
3. Use the water left on the palette to dissolve the color.

2

3

水と絵具が適量，クリムソンレーキー本来の発色になる。

The correct amount of water and paint — The real color of Crimson Lake.

溶く水の量を多くすると，色は薄く，明るくなる。

Dissolved in more water, the color becomes weak and light.

水が多すぎて絵具が少ないため，クリムソンレーキー本来の発色にならない。

Too much water and not enough paint — the real color of Crimson Lake can not be achieved.

絵具が多すぎて，極端に水が少ないため，不透明色になっている。

Too much paint and not enough water — the color becomes opaque.

パレット上の混色
Mixing Colors on the Palette

　彩色のときにチューブから出した色そのままでは鮮やか（高彩度）すぎるため，混色で中間色をつくるケースが多くなる。パレット上の混色とは"低彩度色をつくる"と考えたほうがよい。また，透明水彩は濡れてるうちは色が濃く見えるが，乾くといくらか淡い色になる性質がある。絵具を溶くときは，これを踏まえて，絵具と水の量を加減するとよい。

It is very common for the paint straight from the tube to be too bright for the job in hand and when this is the case, it can be mixed with another color on the palette to produce a mid-tone. When mixing on the palette, think of it as 'making a tint with a low color saturation.' A transparent watercolor may look quite dark when it is wet but it becomes considerably lighter as it dries and this should be born in mind when deciding how much water to use to dissolve a color.

混色専用として，ひんぱんに使うカドミウムイエローライトとバーミリオン，カドミウムレッドディープの3色はパレットの左側に配列しておくと便利。

It is convenient if you place colors such as Cadmium Yellow, Cadmium Red Deep and Vermilion that are often used in mixing on the left hand side of the palette.

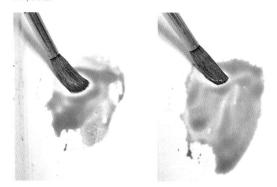

パレット上の混色：最初に溶いた色に混色専用のバーミリオンを混ぜる。絵具と水の加減で色味は変化する。

Mixing on the palette : Mixing a color with Vermilion which is used solely as a mixer. The color changes according to the ratio of water and paint.

混色でつくった色：左は基になる色の割合が多く，右にいくほど混色専用色が多い。

Mixed colors : The color on the left contains a high ratio of the original color while the one right contains a high percentage of the mixer.

基になる色 Original Color		混色専用＝加える色 Mixer Color		つくられた色 Resulting Color						

混色による彩色の例（絵具の割合はチャートの大小で示した）

An example of colors achieved by mixing (The chart shows the ratio of colors).

ウインザーグリーン
Windsor Green

パーマネント
グリーン
Permanent Green

カドミウム
イエロー
Cadmium Yellow

カドミウム
レッド
Cadmium Red

＋

カドミウムイエロー
Cadmium Yellow

＋

カドミウムレッド
Cadmium Red

パーマネント
グリーン
Permanent Green

＋

カドミウム
イエロー
Cadmium Yellow

＋

カドミウム
レッド
Cadmium Red

プルッシアン
ブルー
Prussian Blue

＋

カドミウム
レッド
Cadmium Red

ウルトラ
マリーン
Ultramarine

＋

カドミウム
レッド
Cadmium Red

＋

オリーブ
グリーン
Olive Green

セルリアンブルー
Cerulean Blue

＋

バーミリオン
Vermilion

15

水彩用紙
Paper for Watercolors

ドーサのしっかりした用紙：水分を吸収しないため扱いやすく，平塗りや滲みも楽にできる（ワットマン細目使用）。

Paper With Strong Sizing : This is very easy to use as it does not absorb much water and is ideally suited to techniques such as Washes and Wet-in-Wet (Using fine Watman.)

ドーサの弱い用紙：水分を吸収するため，滲みや平塗りには不向き。吸収されてできるタッチを生かす早描きに向く（パミス細目使用）。

Paper With Weak Sizing : As this absorbs the water readily, it is not suitable for Washes or Wet-in-Wet. The lightest strokes produce bright colors and so it is ideal for pictures which are painted rapidly to show the brush-strokes. (Using fine Pumice)

水彩用紙は表面の紙の目の粗密によって，粗目，中目，細目があり，水の吸収を防ぐため，ドーサといって，にかわ質のものを表面に塗って描きやすいように加工している。発色や塗り重ねによる耐久性は，紙目とドーサの加減によって左右される。

粗目 ドーサの強い紙は，発色が素晴らしいが，絵の具をはじく性質がある。絵の具をじっくり紙になじませて描き込むとき，滲みをたっぷり利かせたいときに使用するとよい。例えば，アルシュ，クラシコファブリアーノ，スリーA，ワットマンなどの粗目がこれに該当する。

中目 ドーサの弱い紙は，前者に比べると発色は劣るが，絵の具をはじくこともなく塗りやすい紙である。風景を現場で短時間に描き上げたいとき，のびのびしたタッチで花や風景を描くとき，下描きの線を生かして淡彩であっさり仕上げるときなどに向いている。マメードリップル，ミューズタッチ，アルシュ，クラシコファブリアーノなどの中目がある。

細目 ドーサの弱い紙は，素早く塗っても定着するし，塗り重ねを何度も繰り返して描き込むことができて使いやすい。THサンダース，ワットマンなどの細目がある。

Paper can be divided into three groups, rough, medium or fine depending on the texture of the surface. In order to stop the paper from soaking up too much water, it is often sized using a mixture of alum and glue. The brilliance of the colors or the durability of the paper after it has been overpainted is affected by the strength of the sizing and the texture of the paper.

Rough Texture With Strong Sizing : This produces marvelously bright colors but it tends to repel the paint. As the paint is absorbed slowly it allows a great deal of control when using such techniques as Blending or Wet-in-Wet. Arches, Classico Fabriano, Three A and Whatman with a rough grain.

Medium Texture With Weak Sizing : Although the colors are not as vivid as in the previously mentioned combination, it does not repel the paint and is easy to work with. It is ideal for painting a landscape on location when time is of an essence, for painting flowers or landscapes with easy strokes, or when producing a picture with delicate coloring that makes use of the original outline strokes. Examples of medium texture papers are, Mermaid Ripple, Muse Touch, Arches, Classico Fabriano, etc.

Fine Texture With Weak Sizing : Even the quickest of strokes can be painted on this kind of paper and it is ideal for Overpainting. T H Saunders and Watman etc. with a fine grain.

水彩紙は，1枚売りのシート，スケッチブック，20枚位を重ねて1枚ずつ使うブロックのものといろいろなタイプがある。

Papers for watercolor painting can be bought by the sheet, in a pad or in a block of about twenty sheets.

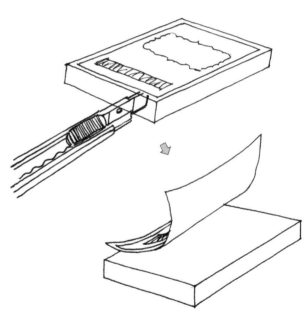

ブロック型はカッターで切り離すと新しい紙面がでる。

In the case of a block, if the top sheet is cut off after the painting is completed, a new sheet will appear ready for work.

スケッチブック
Sketchbook

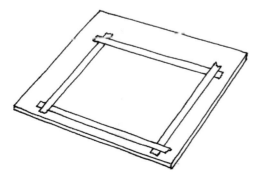

シートは好みのサイズに裁断し，4辺をマスキングテープで画板の手前へ止めて描く。

In the case of a sketchbook or separate sheet, the paper can be cut to size and then fastened to a drawing board with masking tape ready for painting.

筆とタッチ
Brushes and Brushstrokes

筆のタッチ：筆圧の強弱と画面に対しての角度によって，いろいろなタッチが作り出せる。また，筆に含ませる絵具と水の加減によってもタッチは微妙に変わる。

Brushstrokes : Various different kinds of texture can be achieved in the brushstrokes depending on the pressure applied to the brush and its angle to the paper. The amount of paint and water on the brush also adds minute variation to the texture.

筆は 3 本揃えれば十分。左から14号，8号，面相筆 4 号（原寸大）。

Three brushes are sufficient. From the left number 14, number 8, number 4 feature brush (actual size)

18

サイズと材質 筆は丸筆と平筆の2種類あって，太さを号数で表示している。数字が大きいほど太くなっている。穂先の材質は人工のナイロン製と動物製のものがある。動物製は羊，りす，狸，高級品のセーブルといろいろあるが，コリンスキー（シベリアてん）が最高級の筆である。

筆を揃える 透明水彩は水で簡単に洗えるので，色を替えても描き進められる利点がある。高価格になるが，できるだけ良い筆を選び，用途別に各1本揃えれば十分だろう。基本的な彩色用に14〜16号の太い丸筆を1本。細部の描写用に6〜8号の丸筆を1本。それに木の枝などさらに細かい描写用に4号の面相筆（穂先が長めのもの）を加え，都合3本揃えると十分である。

Size and Material: Brushes come in numerous different shapes, sizes and materials. The two basic shapes are flat and round. The thickness is expressed by a number, the higher the number, the thicker the brush. The hair can be made of nylon or animal hair. The most common types of hair are sheep, squirrel and racoon dog, the more expensive being sable and the highest quality Kolinsky (Siberian Ermine).

Buy a Complete Set of Brushes: An advantage of watercolors is that the brush can be easily washed in water and used again immediately for a different color. It is a good idea to buy a complete set of brushes using the best material possible and although this may seem a little extravagant, it must be remembered that only one brush of each type is needed. You basically only need three brushes to begin with, one large round brush (number 14-16) for basic coloring, one narrow round brush (number 6-8) for delicate work and one fine feature brush (one with long hairs) number 4 for more delicate work such as painting branches etc.

細い線は小指で支えて描くとよい。

The thin line is produced by supporting the hand with the little finger.

丸筆14号のタッチ：太さは筆圧の強弱でいろいろできる。

Brushstrokes with a number 14 brush : The thickness is decided by the pressure on the brush.

上から下への運筆

Painted from top to bottom.

下から上への運筆

Painted from bottom to top.

パレット上で穂を押しつぶしバラバラに
して描く。林の繁みや木目の材質感に応
用できる。

The tip of the brush has been splayed by pressing
it hard against the palette before use. This is a
useful technique for painting the foliage in woods
or the wood grain in timber.

上から下への運筆

Painted from top to bottom.

穂を指ではさんでバラバラにして描くと
草むらに応用できる。

Squeezing the hairs of the brush between the
finger and thumb when painting is a useful way to
achieve the texture of grass.

下から上への運筆

Painted from bottom to top.

ドライブラシ：絵具を含ませた筆の水分を布に吸い取らせて，描くとかすれる。キラキラ光る水面やざらついた材質感に応用。

Dry Brush : After the brush has been filled with paint, the water is soaked into a piece of cloth so when it is drawn over the paper, the color breaks up. This technique is good for achieving effects like sunlight on water or rough surface textures.

面相筆のタッチ：細い線は絵具を余り含ませないで，小指で支えて描くとよい。下から上へスピードをつけて引き小枝に応用。

Strokes with the features brush : When painting a thin line, you do not need much paint and it is useful to support the brush with the little finger. Drawn speedily from bottom to top — this is useful for drawing twigs and small branches.
Drawn from the top to the joint with one stroke — this is useful for expressing small trees.

描くときの画材と用具

Equipment to be Used When Painting

画面の角度 水で溶いた絵具は，画面の上を微妙に動くので，平らにして描くことが望ましい。しかし，画面全体を見ながら描き進めるには都合が悪いので，角度が変えられる製図用の机を少し傾斜させて使うと便利だろう。

ヘアドライヤーの効用 ヘアドライヤーは透明水彩の室内制作に欠かせない便利な道具である。彩色した画面を早く乾かすときに使えるし，またタイミングよく画面に当て，滲みやぼかしの進行状態を効果的なところでとめることもできる。画面から20センチ位離し，乾かす箇所に温風をまんべんなく当て，乾きがムラにならないように使うのがコツ。

The Angle of Papers : When using transparent watercolors, the color tends to move slightly on the paper due to the water content flowing and therefore ideally the paper should be laid flat to keep this to a minimum. However, if the paper is flat, it is difficult to look at both the subject and the work in process simultaneously so most artists prefer to keep the paper at a slight angle. A draftsman's drawing board is ideal as the angle can be altered freely and if an easel is used, one which allows the angle to be changed is best.

The use of a hairdryer : A hairdryer is a very useful piece of equipment when working indoors. Not only can it be used to dry a painted area quickly, but it can also be used to control the extent of Washes and Blending. Hold the dryer about 20 centimeters from the work and play the hot air evenly over the whole area to be dried. It is important to ensure that the drying does not create an unevenness in the tone.

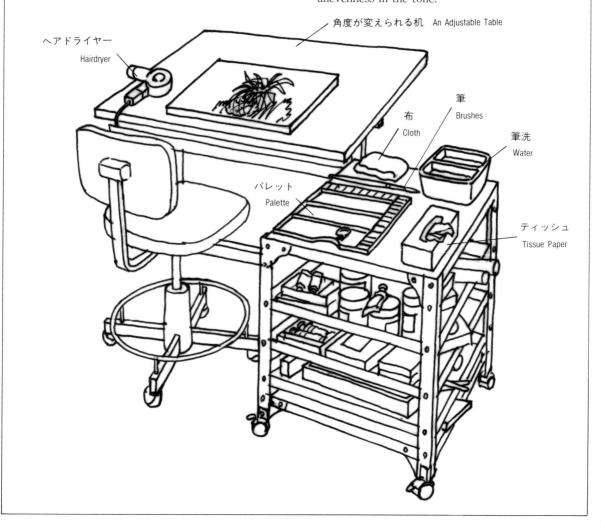

ヘアドライヤー Hairdryer

角度が変えられる机 An Adjustable Table

布 Cloth

筆 Brushes

筆洗 Water

パレット Palette

ティッシュ Tissue Paper

2　章

彩色の基本

Chapter 2

Basic Coloring

重ね塗りの効果
Overpainting

　下に塗った色を完全に乾かしてから新たに透明色を重ねると，2色が透けて混じり合い，透明水彩ならではの色彩効果が生まれる。この技法は，塗り重ねる色よりも，明るい色を下に塗ることを基本にするとよい。

　異なった2色を重ねて別の色をつくったり，同系色を重ねて微妙な変化を求めることも可能だが，透明水彩はフレッシュさが生命，重ね過ぎは発色効果を損なってしまうので避けること。また，下地が乾いていても同じ部分を何度も塗り直していると下の色が溶けだして混ざり合い，濁ってしまうので計画性を必要とする。

One of the special characteristics of transparent watercolors is that after one color has dried, another color can be painted over it, the two colors blending. This is known as 'Overpainting' but it must be remembered that light colors cannot be painted over dark colors so the light colors must be painted first.
Two different colors can be painted over each other to produce a new color or two tones of the same color can be used to produce a gentle graduation. However, one must bear in mind that the freshness of the colors is one of the most important characteristics of watercolor paints and if the same area is overpainted too often, this will be impaired. Also, even if the first color has completely dried, if it is overpainted repeatedly, it will dissolve and produce a muddy finish so you must plan before using this technique.

透明水彩の場合
Using Transparent Watercolors.

明るい色を塗って乾かす。

Paint a light color and allow it to dry.

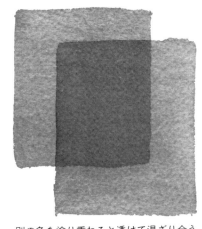

別の色を塗り重ねると透けて混ざり合う。

Paint another color over it and the two colors mix, the first being seen through the second.

不透明水彩（ガッシュ）の場合
Using Non-transparent Paints (Gouache).

色を塗り乾かす。

Paint the first color and allow it to dry.

塗り重ねた色は変わらない。

Paint a second color over this, and it will not change.

重ね塗りの効果：必ず下の色を完全に乾かしてから重ねること。

To Achieve the Best Effect : The first color must be allowed to completely dry before applying the second color.

明るい色を下にすること。

The lighter color must be painted first.

一方が暗すぎても効果はでない。

If one of the colors is too dark, the desired effect may not be achieved.

暗い色どうしは効果はでない。

If both colors are dark, they will not mix.

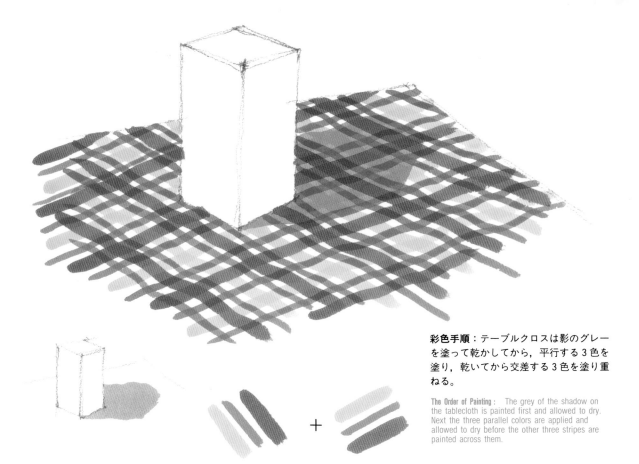

彩色手順：テーブルクロスは影のグレーを塗って乾かしてから，平行する 3 色を塗り，乾いてから交差する 3 色を塗り重ねる。

The Order of Painting : The grey of the shadow on the tablecloth is painted first and allowed to dry. Next the three parallel colors are applied and allowed to dry before the other three stripes are painted across them.

透けてみえる題材を描いた例：奥にあるびん，レモンの順に仕上げ，最後に手前のコップを塗り重ねる。

Painting Transparent Objects : Paint the bottle in the background first, then the lemon and leave the glass in the foreground to last.

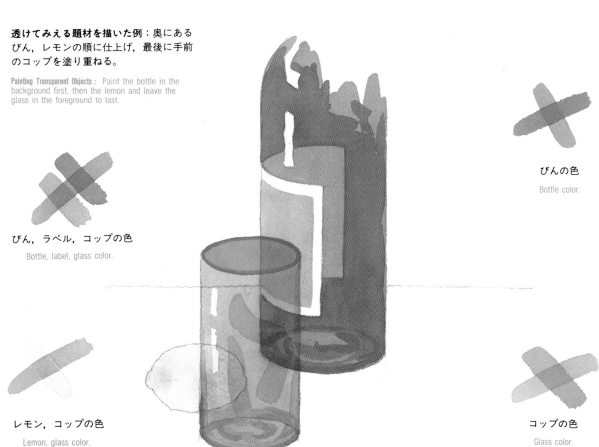

びん，ラベル，コップの色

Bottle, label, glass color.

びんの色

Bottle color.

レモン，コップの色

Lemon, glass color.

コップの色

Glass color.

25

平塗り
Flat Wash

平塗りは空や水面，あるいは人物や静物の背景を塗るときに，よく使われる基本的な技法なので，しっかりマスターしておこう。

平塗りをムラなく，きれいに仕上げるコツは筆に絵具をたっぷりつけてから，画面に軽くあてて塗ることだ。絵具の含みが少ないと，筆を画面に強くこすりつけてしまうのでムラができるし，絵具の発色効果も損なわれてしまう。

塗るときは，できるだけ太めの筆を用いて，のびのびした大きな筆運びを心がけて欲しい。

A Flat Wash is often used for the sky, water, as well as the background of portraits and still life. It is a basic technique and should be thoroughly mastered. The secret to producing a nice even Flat Wash is to put a generous amount of paint on the brush and move it lightly over the paper. If there is not enough paint, it becomes necessary to press the brush hard onto the paper causing unevenness and a loss of color. The effect is best achieved by using the largest brush possible and moving it in large, even strokes.

良い塗り方：筆が少し曲がる程度だとムラなくきれいにできる。

Good technique : If the brush bends slightly as it is being drawn over the paper, it will produce good, even results.

悪い塗り方：筆を紙に押しつけて塗るとムラになる。

Bad Technique : If the brush is pressed too heavily onto the paper it will produce an uneven result.

平塗りの練習：慣れるまでは塗るスペースより多めに溶いた絵具を筆にたっぷり含ませ練習しよう。筆は画面から離さず，一定のスピードで塗るとよい。ここでは左右の筆運びで一気に塗ってるが，上下，斜めいろいろな方向から練習してみよう。

Wash Practice : Until you become used to this technique, it is best to mix more paint than is necessary for the area to be covered and to put a lot on the brush. Making sure that the brush does not leave the surface of the paper, make your strokes at a steady pace. In this example we are painting from left to right, but you should also practice doing it vertically and diagonally until you are competent in any direction.

静物のバックを塗る：右利きは左下から
塗り始めるとよい。ものとバックの境目
を塗ってから広いスペースに移るが，葉
や茎の細かい隙間は最後に塗る。

Painting the Background to Still-Life : Right-handed
people should start by painting from bottom left.
Start with the border of the objects then move on
to the larger spaces although the narrow spaces
between the leaves or stalks should be left until
last.

滲みの効果
Wet-in-Wet

先に塗った色が濡れている上に次の色を重ねると色が滲んで，水彩特有の彩色効果を作り出してくれる。表現に迷って筆が進まなくなったときは，滲みを利用すると意外にうまくいくこともある便利で頼りになる技法だ。

下地になる最初の色をたっぷり塗っておき，上に重ねて滲み込ませるときは筆の水分を少なめにしておくのがコツ。この絵具と水の量の配分を逆にすると，上に重ねたタッチの跡がはっきり残ってしまい，滲みというよりシミのようになってしまうので注意しよう。

If a second color is painted over another which is still wet, the two colors will blend to form an effect unique to watercolors. This technique can be used to surprising effect when one is not sure how to continue with a painting and therefore it is a very useful skill to master.
The secret is to give an apply coating of the first color, but to cut down on the amount of water in the second color. If the opposite ratio of water is used, the second color will not blend well into the first and will cause a stain rather than an gradation.

1

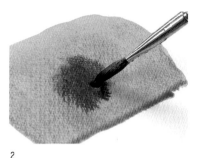

2

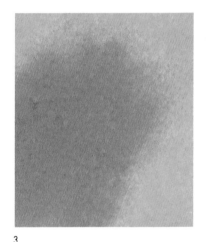

3

滲みの練習：たっぷり塗った色が濡れている上に(1)，さらにたっぷり色を重ねると(2)，柔らかく滲みが広がる(3)。

Wet-in-Wet Practice : First apply an even coat of wet paint (1) then add a good amount of a second color (2) and the two will blend to produce a new color (3)

滲みのコントロール：水分を少なくした筆で滲みを行うと，滲みはあまり広がらずきれいにできる。

Controlling the Spread of Color : If you add a second color without much water content, it will not spread much and will produce a good result.

滲みの失敗例：重ねる色の水の量が多すぎると色と色の境目がくっきりシミのような跡になる。

Bad Technique : The second color contained too much water which resulted in a stain around the borders.

木：明るいグリーンを塗り，濡れてるう
ちに暗い色をつけ陰を滲ませて変化をつ
ける。

Trees : Paint the foliage in a light green and while
this is still wet, add some darker color. This will
represent the shadow and produce a more
interesting result.

空：全体を水で湿らせておいて，雲の形
を残して塗ると柔らかな表現になる。

Sky : Wet the entire area with water first then
paint in the blue, leaving the area of the clouds.
The paint will run giving a nice soft feeling.

土：グリーンの上に土の色を
滲ませ，露出した感じを表現
する。

Ground : Paint the green of the grass
first then blend in the brown of the
earth. This will provide a very
natural effect.

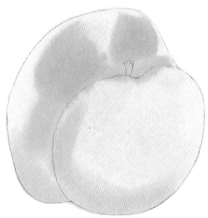

模様を滲ませる：ネープルスイエローを桃全体に塗り，濡れている上に模様になるクリムソンレーキを塗り重ねて滲ませる。

Blending a Pattern：Paint the whole peach using Naples Yellow then while it is still wet, blend in the pattern using Crimson Lake.

良い例：陰影を描かなくても絵画的には成功する。

Good Technique：Even without painting the shadow, it succeeds from an artistic point of view.

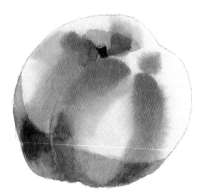

悪い例：陰を描くと色合いを損なう。

Bad Technique：The color has been lost by adding the shadow.

グレーの混色　Mixed Grey

エメラルドグリーン　　　　　クリムソンレーキ

Emerald Green　　　　　　Crimson Lake

絵具の量によって，冷たいグリーンがかったグレーや暖かい紫がかったグレーになる。

Depending on the ratios of paint you can achieve anything from a cool green/grey to a warm purple/ grey.

滲みと陰影：果物は色合いが微妙なので，光と陰の色を描き分けるのは難しい。滲みを使った場合，光の当たった部分と陰の境界を処理することはとくに難しく，失敗も多くなる。下に落ちる影をあっさり描く程度にしたほうが絵画的に美しく仕上がる。

Blending and Shadow : The colors of fruit are very delicate and it is difficult to bring out the differences of light and shade. When using Wet-in-Wet it is particularly difficult to bring out the border between the light and shadow, and it is very easy to make a mistake. If the shadows falling at the bottom are drawn simply, it will give a beautiful, artistic finish.

表面が粉を吹いたような果物は，下地のグレーを混色でつくり模様の色を滲ませる。

For fruit that has a natural coating of powder on the surface, use grey for a base color and then blend the pattern color into it.

全面にグレーを塗る。　　乾かないうちに色を滲ませる。

Paint the whole surface grey then before it dries, blend in the color.

ぼかし塗り
Gradated Wash

　濃い色から薄い色へ，あるいは明から暗へ調子を徐々にぼかしていくこの方法は応用する機会も多いので，しっかり習得しておこう。平塗りよりはいくぶん難しくなるが，何度か試してみると慣れるし，コツものみこめるはずだ。

　平塗りと同様，画面が濡れてる間に塗りすすめる技法で，水の加減が大切になる。例えば濃い色から段々に明るくしていく場合，あらかじめ明るくするところを水で湿しておくと，絵具が自然ににじんでいくので簡単にぼかしができる。

It is common to have dark colors flow gradually into lighter ones and shade into bright so this is another important technique to learn. It is a little harder than the wash technique, but it is not too difficult to master with practice. As with the Wash, it should be done while the paper is wet and control of the amount of water used is very important. For instance, when painting a dark color going into light, if the area where the light color will fall is moistened first, the paint will naturally flow that way making it easy to produce a gradation.

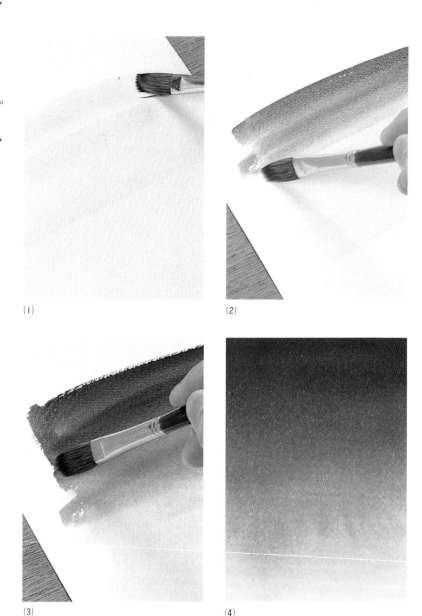

(1)　(2)　(3)　(4)

ぼかし塗りの練習(明から暗へ)：最初に塗った明るい色が(1)，乾かないうちに中間の色を塗り(2)，最後に暗い色を塗る(3)。のびのびした筆運びをすることが大切。

Graded Wash practice (from light to dark): The mid (2) and dark tones (3) should be painted before the light tone (1) has a chance to dry. It is important that these colors are all applied with good steady strokes.

(1)

(2)

(3)

空と山のぼかし塗り：山との境目の明るい空の色は，山の部分へはみ出して塗り（1），きわを湿った筆で撫でてぼかしておくと，次に山を描くときにきれいにできる（2）。山の色も空と同様，次に塗る山の部分へはみ出して塗っておくとよい（3）。

Shading the area between the mountains and sky: The light sky color that falls next to the mountain should be painted first and allowed to intrude on the mountain area (1). The borderline can then be softened by gentle strokes with a wet brush and then the mountain can be painted (2). The same is true for both the mountain colors and the sky color, they should be allowed to intrude into the area of the next mountain to be painted (3).

ぼかしとタッチ
Blending and Brushstrokes

色面が湿っているときに塗り重ねると，筆の跡（タッチ）はソフトにぼけるが，乾いた色面に塗り重ねた場合，タッチがはっきり表れる。これが強すぎて気になるときは，水を含ませたた筆でヘリ（エッジ）を撫でてソフトにぼかしながら描くとよい。

タッチをそのまま生かすときは，どんな用紙でも構わない。しかし，ぼかすときは，良い用紙（言い方を変えれば，高価な紙ということになる）を使ったほうがうまくいく。つまり良い用紙ほど丈夫でドーサのムラもないので，なんべん色面をこすっても，透明感や発色を損なうことはない。

If a paint is applied on top of wet paint, the brushstroke will blend and soften but if applied to dry paint, it will remain clear. If this clear stroke is unwanted, it can be softened by feathering the edge with a brush filled with water. If you want the brushstrokes to remain clear, any paper will suffice, but if you wish to soften the brushstrokes, it is best to use good (expensive) paper. This is because the better papers are strong and have an even coating of size so no matter how often you work at the surface, the color and transparency of the paints will not be affected.

滲ませる：最初は個々のモチーフの色が混ざり合っても構わない。滲みの技法を使って描いていく。

Blend : In the beginning, it does not matter if the colors of the individual items run into each other so the Wet-in-Wet technique should be utilized.

タッチをぼかす
Blurring a Brushstroke

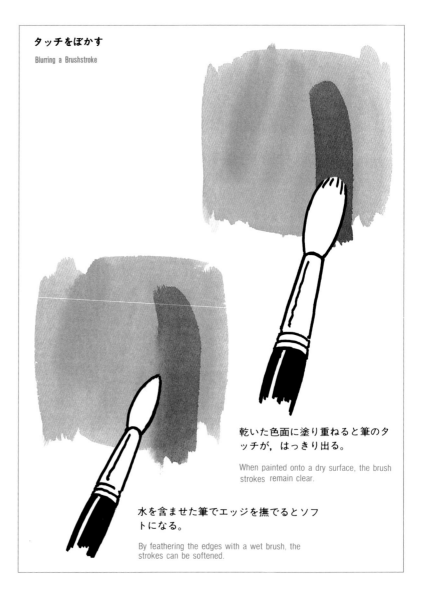

乾いた色面に塗り重ねると筆のタッチが，はっきり出る。

When painted onto a dry surface, the brush strokes remain clear.

水を含ませた筆でエッジを撫でるとソフトになる。

By feathering the edges with a wet brush, the strokes can be softened.

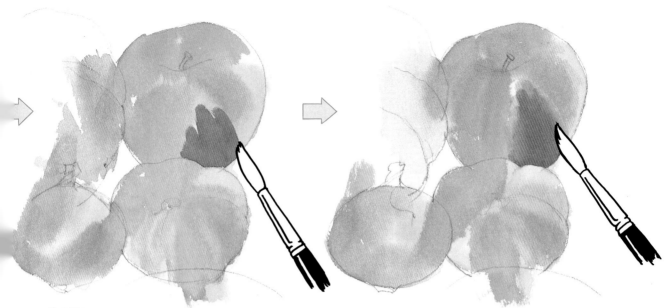

塗り重ねる：滲ませた明るい色を乾かし
てから暗い色を重ねる。

Overpainting : After the lighter, blended colors have
dried, Overpaint with the darker colors.

ぼかす：色の境目が，くっきりついた部
分は水で湿らせた筆で撫でてぼかす。

Gradated Wash : Use a brush with water on it to blur
the edges of the areas where there is a distinct
division between the colors.

リンゴやトマトは滑らかな肌合いをだすため，タッチをぼか
したが，カボチャやジャガイモはゴツゴツした感じを表すた
めタッチを生かしている。

In the case of the apple or tomato, the surface was allowed to blend to give
the smooth feeling of the skin, while the brush-strokes were allowed to
remain on the pumpkin and potato to give an impression of the rough texture
of the skin.

吸い取り
Blotting

色面が濡れている間にティッシュで吸い取り，複雑で変化のある調子をつくりだす技法だ。ただ平塗りをしただけの部分でも，ティッシュを押し当てる力の加減で，かなり変化のある調子がつくりだせる。

また，石垣，屋根，窓など同じ形のものがたくさん集まって，単調になりがちな対象を描く場合，画面上の変化をつける有効な技法となる。

If the paint is blotted with tissue paper while it is still wet, it will produce some interstesting tone effects. Even a plain wash can be changed by blotting it with tissue paper to produce quite a different effect, the amount of pressure used governing the change in tone. Where there are a number of objects of the same shape such as stone walls, roofs, windows, etc. This technique can be used to provide an interesting diversity.

吸い取りで樹肌に変化をつける。

Using blotting to produce texture in trees:

１　平塗りで木を描く。

1. Use the wash technique to paint the tree.

２　乾かないうちにティッシュで吸い取り変化をつける。

2. Use tissue paper to blot the paint before it dries to produce variety.

３　乾かしてから描き込む。

3. After the paint has dried, fill in the detail.

空：空全体を塗り，乾かないうちにティッシュで吸い取る。明るい箇所は強く，陰になる箇所は弱く押しつけ，変化をつける。

Sky: Paint the whole sky, then before the paint has dried, blot it with tissue paper. Pressing hard will produce lighter areas while pressing more gently will produce darker areas making the picture more interesting.

窓：最初は明るめの色を塗り，吸い取る。乾いてから暗い色を重ね，吸い取る。この繰り返しで変化をつけ，同じような窓の並んだ対象を描くとき画面が単調になるのを救う。

Windows: First paint a light color then blot it. After the paint has dried, apply a darker color on top and blot that too.
Repeating this process will produce interesting tones and in a subject where there are rows of similar windows, it will add interest to the picture.

 ⇨  ⇨

洗い出し
Diluting

透明水彩は，明るい色から着色するのが基本で，その逆は発色の効果を損ない失敗につながってしまう。ここでは暗い色を塗ってしまった後にハイライトをいれたり，画面を洗って部分的に描き直しをする技法を解説しよう。

なおこの洗い出しは，アルシュ紙やファブリアーノ紙のようにドーサ（紙の表面に塗ってるしみこみ防止剤）の強い紙（指で触ると堅い）は，絵具が紙にしっかり食い込んでいるので難しくなる。

When using transparent water colors, the basic technique is to start with the lighter colors then fill in the daker ones later.
If it is not done in this way, it will be difficult to produce the lighter tones. However, you decide later that you wish to add a highlight to a darker area you have already painted, it is possible to dilute the color.
This technique will not be successful on strongly glazed paper, Such as Arche or Fabriano (paper that has been coated to prevent the pigments from soaking into it and which are hard to the touch) as the paint will stick to the paper.

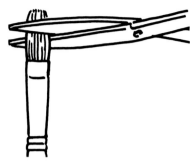

洗いだし用筆：油彩用の豚毛の平筆かナイロン筆（４～６号）の穂先を１センチ位の長さに切り揃える。

For the best results use a flat, pig hair or nylon brush (4-6 oil-paint type) and cut the bristles to a length of about 1 cm.

(1)

１　修正する部分を水をたっぷり含ませた筆でこする。
２　溶け出した色をティッシュで吸い取る。
３　乾いてから加筆修正する。

1. Rub the area to be corrected with a lot of water on the brush.
2. Use tissue paper to soak up the paint as it is disolved.
3. After it has dried make the necessary corrections.

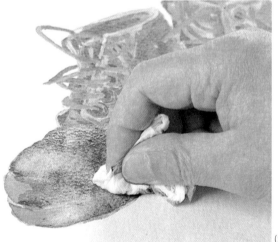

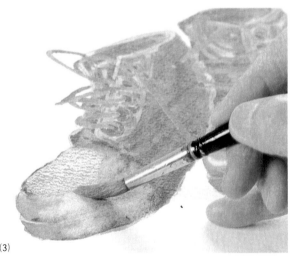

(2)　(3)

修正する前の絵

The image before making necessary corrections.

ハイライトをいれる部分的を水を含ませた細い筆でこする。

When adding highlights, use a narrow brush with plenty of water on it.

ティッシュで色を吸い取り明るくする。

Then soak up the paint with tissue paper.

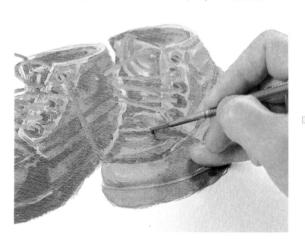

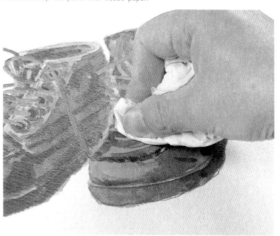

重ね塗りによる制作手順
The Order In Which Paint Should Be Applied

完成図

Finished Painting

建物の立体感は，塗り重ねた部分と塗り残した下の色で，シャープな境界をつくって日なたと日陰を描き分けて表す。明るい日なたの色を建物全体に塗り，乾かしてから日陰の色を塗り重ねると，強い日差しの下での建物の感じが表現できる。この塗り重ねの技法と滲みを併用しながら，計画的な手順で彩色することで，色に微妙な変化と深みをあたえ透明水彩の魅力は発揮される。

When painting buildings, a feeling of depth can be achieved by creating a sharp division between the basic color and the colors that are Overpainted, producing the feeling of the sun hitting the structure. First paint the entire building using the light color and once this has dried, Overpaint to produce the shadows, creating a feeling of strong sunlight. Using a combination of Overpainting and Wet-in-Wet, adding colors in a carefully planned order, a variety in colors and depth can be achieved that brings out the best of the watercolor medium.

1，画板にマスキングテープで固定した用紙に，芯の軟らかい鉛筆で濃くはっきり下描きをする。

1. Fix the paper to the drawing board with masking tapes and fill in the outlines clearly and heavily with a soft pencil.

下描きは，色が重なっていく過程で形が分かりにくくならないように，濃くはっきりした線で描いておく。また下描きの段階で陰影をつけてしまうと，透明水彩特有の発色効果を損なってしまうため，鉛筆で調子をつけずに輪郭線のみを描写すること。下描きとは "着彩するときの目安になる境界線" という認識をもつとよい。

It can become difficult to see the finer details of the subject when several coats of paint have been applied so make the pencil lines of the sketch firm and dark. If shadowing is applied on the sketch, it will show through the paint, spoiling the effect of the watercolor, so only draw the outlines and leave the toning until later. It is important to remember that the sketch is "Only to be an outline to act as a guide when coloring."

2，彩色は明るい色から始める。　2. Start with the light colors.

透明色の重ね塗りで，色に深み
をもたせる描き方の場合，下地は
明るい色を平塗りしておこう。乾
かしてから次の色を重ねていくの
が基本だが，部分的に滲みを使い，
乾かしてからさらに塗り重ね，微
妙な効果をねらってみてもおもし
ろい。

If you want to show the depth of
the colors when Overpainting, it is
best to apply the base colors as a
Flat Wash. Although the basic
technique calls for the paints to
have dried before starting the next
coat, it is sometimes interesting if
you allow the later colors to blend
into the earlier ones (Wet-in-Wet)
then go over them again after
they have dried. This technique
permits very delicate changes in
tone.

中景の緑は前景より低彩度にする。

Use a green with a lower color saturation in the middle distance than the
one used in the front.

建物は明るい色を塗り，部分的に滲みを使う。

Paint the buildings with light colors and allow them to blend in places.

3，屋根瓦は，単調なパターンになるのを避け滲みの効果を利用。

3. In order to stop the roof tiles from forming a monotonous pattern, wet-in-wet was utilized.

屋根の滲みを乾かしてから，瓦の陰影を大まかにつける。

After the paint has dried the shadows of the tiles can be added roughly.

　前景，中景は平塗り，部分的に滲みを併用して描き進めているが，まだ平面的な彩色段階だ。立体感をつける陰影表現はこの後の仕事になる。

We have now filled in the front and middle distance using Flat Wash and Wet-in-Wet techniques, but the picture is still very flat. Shadows will be added to give the picture depth later.

4，壁面が乾いてから建物の陰の色を塗り重ねる。

4. After the paint of the walls has dried, the shade and shadow can be Overpainted.

　陰影の色は，パレット上の混色でつくった透明なグレーを使う。先に塗った壁面の色が乾いてから重ねていくが，軽く塗らないと，絵具に含まれた水が作用して下の色が溶けだすこともある。すばやく一気に塗るのがコツだ。

The shadows should be painted using a transparent grey that is mixed on the palette first. It should be applied after the color of the walls has dried but this must be done lightly, or the water in the paint will loosen the first color and cause it to blend. The secret is to paint quickly with a minimum of strokes.

パレット上で混色したグレーを塗り重ねる。

Overpainting with a grey that has been mixed on the palette.

緑の陰影は，単調なパターンにならないように絵具を溶く水加減と筆のタッチを微妙に変えて塗り重ねていく。

In order to stop the shadow in the green from becoming monotonous, it should be Overpainted with differing amounts of water on the brush and different pressure on the brush when making the strokes.

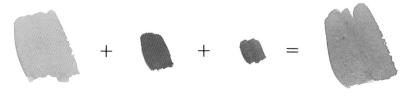

パレット上の混色でつくった陰のグレー。

The grey for the shadow that was mixed on the palette.

重ね塗りによる制作手順　The Order In Which Paint Should Be Applied

5，空の上に重ね塗りする遠景の樹木は最後に描く。
繁みの陰影の濃淡は水加減で微妙な違いを表す。

5. The trees that are painted over the sky should be left until the last. Shades and shadows can be added to the undergrowth by varying the amount of water used.

空は雲を残し平塗りで一気に描く。

The sky is painted using a Flat Wash, leaving the areas for the clouds.

雲は滲みの効果を利用するので，空のブルーが乾かないうちにパレット上で混色したグレーで陰になる部分を描く。空が完全に乾いてから遠景の濃いグリーンを塗り重ねて完成とする（40ページ参照）。

Before the blue of the sky has dried, use the grey that you have mixed on the palette to fill in the shadows of the clouds. After the sky has completely dried, fill in the dark green in the distance and the picture is complete. (see page 40)

45

透明と不透明の比較
The Difference Between Transparent and Opaque Paints

透明水彩の場合　Transparent colors

白い花はバックを塗り用紙の白地を生かす。

White flower : Fill in the background and leave the white of the paper for the flower.

明るいピンクの花　Pale Pink Flower

パーマネントローズを水で薄め，明度を調節する。

Water down some Permanent Rose to achieve the desired color.

薄めたピンクを塗る。

Apply the lightened pink.

湿った筆で中心部を撫でてぼかす。

Use a brush with water on it to form a light gradation towards the center.

乾かしてから花芯と陰を描く。

When the paint has dried fill in the shadow and stamen.

暗いピンクの花　Dark Pink Flower

パーマネント
ローズ

Permanent Rose

+

マゼンタ

Magenta

=

花芯を描いてから花弁を塗る。

Paint the stamen first then paint in the petals.

花弁が乾かないうちにマゼンタを滲ませる。

Before the petals have dried, blend in some magenta.

乾かしてから陰の色を重ねる。

After the paint has dried, fill in the shadows.

46

不透明水彩（ガッシュ）の場合　Opaque Paints (Gouache)

白い花はバックを塗ってからホワイトで描く。

After painting the background, fill in the white flower with white paint.

明るいピンクの花　Pale Pink Flower

オペラ
Opera

＋

ホワイト
White

＝

混色で作ったピンクを塗る。

Paint the flower using a pink made from mixing Opera and White.

ピンクが乾かないうちにホワイトを塗る。

Before the pink dries, add white.

陰をつけ，花芯を描く。

Add shadows and draw in the stamen.

濃いピンクの花　Dark Pink Flower

濃い色の場合，花芯の部分を塗り残しておく。

In the case of a dark flower, leave the stamen until last.

裏側の明るい色を塗り重ねる。

Overpaint to achieve the lighter color of the petals.

花芯を描く。

Fill in the stamen.

ホワイトの効果
Using White

　透明水彩のホワイトの表現は，紙の白地を生かすことが基本的だが，複雑で小さな対象になると，白地を残すのは技術的に難しくなる。

　このような場合，絵具のホワイトを積極的に使い，自由な筆使いをしたほうがうまくいく。絵具のホワイトは不透明なので，透明色と混色して不透明色をつくり，形を描き起こしていく方法である。部分的に使うので透明水彩としての様式をこわすことはない。

In order to obtain a white when using transparent watercolor the accepted technique is to leave the paper unpainted, but in very small areas, this can be very difficult to achieve. In these situations, white paint should be used freely to achieve the required result. White is not a transparent pigment so it can be mixed with other transparent color to produce non-transparent watercolors which if used sparingly, will not spoil the effect of the painting.

Ⅰ　黄色の上にグリーンをにじませ葉と茎を同時に彩色。

1. Green can be blended in on top of yellow to color both leaves and stalks.

2　バックの濃いブルーを塗ることで葉と茎の形を描き起こす。

2. Paint the dark blue background, leaving the areas of the leaves and stalks.

小さな花は不透明色を使い最終段階で描き起こす。

In the last step, use non-transparent colors to paint small flowers.

3　花を不透明色で描き起こす。白い花はホワイトを溶く
　　水加減で手前(少ない)，奥(多い)の違いを表す。

3. Paint the flowers in non-transparent colors. According to the amount of
water used, the white flowers can be brought to the foreground (less
water) or moved into the back(more water).

マスキングの効果
The Effect of Masking

明るい小さな形や連続模様を塗り残してから彩色するのは，根気がいるし手間もかかる。そんなときはマスキング用材で塗り残す部分を覆って，一気に彩色すると，思いどおりの形が簡単にできる。

マスケットインクを使って描いた花。

A flower painted using masking fluid.

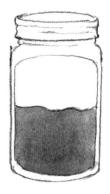

マスケットインク：液状なので，画面に自由な形を筆で描ける。容器のふたをしたまま，よく振って撹拌し，水のようなグレーになってから使う。乾くと筆にこびりついて落ちなくなるので，使い終わった筆はすぐに水洗いすること。

Masking Fluid : Being a fluid, it can be used to create any shape. Shake the bottle well before use to produce a grey water-like liquid. Once the fluid has dried it is very difficult to remove so wash the brush in water immediately after use.

筆にインクをつけて，白く抜きたい形を描く。

Dip the brush in the fluid and draw the object to be masked.

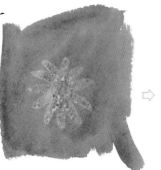

インクを乾かしてから周りの色を塗る。

Once the fluid has dried, paint the surrounding colors.

専用のラバーでインクをこすり取る。

Using a special eraser, remove the fluid.

It is sometimes calls for some very delicate work to leave a small area unpainted and it requires a lot of patience to leave repeating pattern to fill in later, but if these areas are masked first, the color can be applied quite easily without any effort and the area you require will still remain.

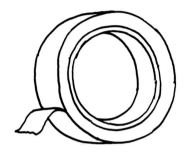

マスキングテープ：細長い形を白抜きするときに便利。

Masking Tape : Useful for producing long, thin white objects.

マスキングテープで覆って描いた景色。

Scenery painted using masking tape.

白く抜きたい形にカッターで切って貼りつける。隙間から絵具が入り込まないように強くこすって貼ること。

Cut out the shape of the object you wish to remain white and stick the tape onto the paper, pressing hard to ensure that no paint can find its way under the tape.

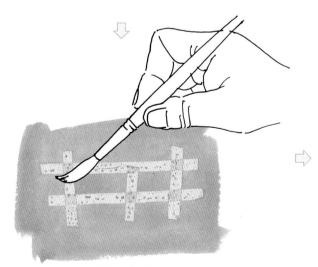

周りの色を塗る。

Paint the surrounding color.

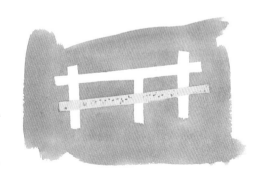

テープはカッターの先で浮かして慎重に剝がす。

Lift a corner of the tape with the point of a cutter and then peel it off very carefully.

51

画面を削る
Scraping Back

ペインティングナイフやカッターを使い，画面をひっかいたり，削ったりして変化をつけ，筆とは異なる絵肌をつくる技法である。岩のようなゴツゴツした固い質感や波しぶきの表現に効果的である。

水面の色が乾いてから，カッターでひっかき白い波を表現する。

Paint the surface of the sea and once it has dried, scrape it with a cutter to get the white of the waves.

重ね塗りした色が濡れている間にペインティングナイフで削る。

After building up the paint, use a painting knife to scrape it before the paint dries.

An interesting effect can be
achieved by using a painting knife
or cutter to scratch or scrape the
surface of the picture. It is
particularly useful for representing
the rough surface of rocks or the
spray of the waves.

筆の弾力を利用して絵具を弾き飛ばす。

Use a stiff brush to spatter paint on the picture.

画面が濡れてるうちに，先の尖ったもの
で強くゆっくりきずをつけると，色が染
み込み細く鋭い滲んだ線ができる。

While the surface is still wet, make a line pressing
down slowly and strongly with a pointed object.
The paint will soak into the depression producing a
thin colored line.

線描を生かす淡彩
Line and Wash

　鉛筆やペンなどの線描を生かす淡彩スケッチは，透明水彩本来の発色のさわやかさが生命である。何度も塗り重ねず，あっさり一気に彩色するのがコツ。線描に使う画材は鉛筆，インク，フェルトペン（油性），あるいは水溶性のフェルトペンも彩色のときに線が滲むのでおもしろい。

The delicate colors of the transparent watercolor are what make or break a Line and Wash picture. The trick is not to paint over the same area several times but do it in one stroke. The lines can be drawn using a pencil, pen or felt pen (oil based), although a water base felt pen can also produce some interesting effects as it will blend with the paints.

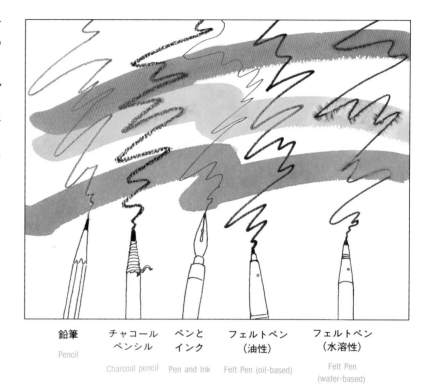

鉛筆	チャコールペンシル	ペンとインク	フェルトペン（油性）	フェルトペン（水溶性）
Pencil	Charcoal pencil	Pen and Ink	Felt Pen (oil-based)	Felt Pen (water-based)

フェルトペン（油性）に彩色　Coloring over a felt pen (oil-based) drawing.

インクに彩色　Coloring over ink.

チャコールペンシルに彩色　Coloring over charcoal pencil.

塩を使う効果
Using Salt

塩が水分を吸う性質を利用すると，
筆では表現できない不思議なパタ
ーンができる。バックや幻想的な
イラストレーションに試してみる
とおもしろいだろう。

Salt can be used to react with the
water in the paint to produce
some very interesting effects.
This technique can be used to
produce backgrounds or
psychedelic pictures.

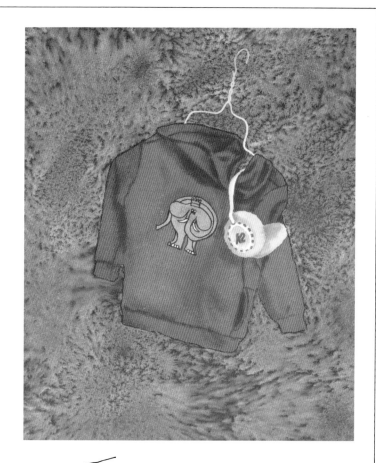

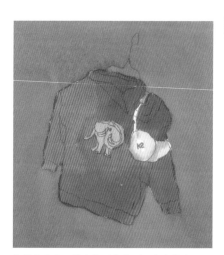

主役を完全に乾かしてからバックを塗る。こ
の技法は画面が濡れているうちに行うので，
バック全体を一気に塗る。

After the main subject has been allowed to
completely dry the background color painted. The
paint has to be wet for this effect to work so the
entire background should be painted at one time.

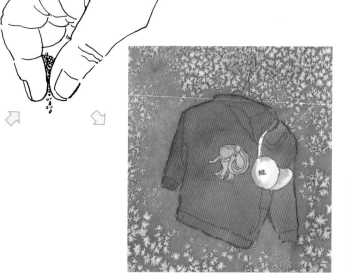

塩をバックに振り撒くと水分を吸って白っぽ
い雪の結晶のような模様ができる。

Sprinkle salt over the background and it will soak
up the water leaving a white pattern like
snowflakes over the background.

3 章
表現と技法

Chapter 3

Expression and Technique

明度対比を生かす　Making Use of Contrast

　いくら色彩がよくても明度対比が明快でないと，あいまいな絵になってしまう。透明水彩の場合，水で薄めると明るい色になるが，それぞれの固有色によっても明度差がある。例えば，イエロー系は明るい色で，暗い色はプルッシアンブルーやセピアである。このことを理解したうえで，明度対比の効果を生かし，画面にメリハリをつけることも絵づくりの大切な要素である。

No matter how well painted a picture may be, if it does not have a good clear contrast, it will remain weak. In the case of transparent watercolors, adding water will make the colors lighter, but the inherent brightness of colors must also be taken into account. For instance, Yellow is a bright color whereas Prussian Blue or Sepia are dark colors. It is important to understand this in order to produce a good lively painting with plenty of contrast.

良い例：日なた側のバックは，明度対比を強くして対象をはっきりさせる。

A Good Example : The light side of the subject contrasts very well with the background making the object stand out.

悪い例：日なたと陰側のバックの明度対比が逆のため，対象の形がはっきりしない。風景画の場合，遠近感というより明度差で前後を区別するという考え方で描くとよい。

Bad Example : The subject does not contrast with the background, making it difficult to see. When painting landscapes use contrast to produce a feeling of depth rather than just relying on perspective.

良い例：日なた側のバックの明度対比を強く，陰側は同じ明度にして，バックに溶け込むようにすると，周り全部をはっきりさせるのと別のおもしろ味がでる。

A Good Example : The light side of the subject contrasts well with the background while the dark side has the same tonal density. This produces an interesting composition and has a different feeling to when the whole subject stands out.

明度対比の良い例　A Good Example of Contrast.

雲は明度差と配置で山を引き立てる要素とする。

The brightness and position of the clouds forces the viewers attention onto the mountains.

主役の山の明度に対比させ，背景の空は明るくする。

In order to make the main subject of the mountains stand out, the sky has been painted light.

手前の草原や中景の木立の明るさに対して，山を暗くする。

The mountains in the rear have been painted darker to contrast them with the plain and trees in the foreground.

明度対比の悪い例　A Bad Example of Contrast.

雲の配置が山の連なりのように見える。

The position of the clouds makes them look like an extension of the mountains.

山が明るく空と明度差がないので，主役が引き立たない。

The mountains are too light and do not contrast with the sky. The subject does not stand out.

陰が強すぎる。繁み全体を背景の山との明度対比で表すこと。

The shadow is too dark. The trees should be made to stand out from the mountains through the use of contrast.

絵づくりのポイント　How To Produce a Picture

絵づくりと明度　Painting and Brightness

前景を強く，遠景を弱くというのが，絵の遠近感を表現するためのセオリーである。しかし，人の目はどんな風景に対しても常に同じ感情を抱くとは限らない。なにを強く描き，目立たせるかは，描く本人が最も興味をもったものにするべきであろう。遠近感にこだわらず，明度対比を生かして，ねらいを明快にした絵づくりも必要である。

When painting a landscape the basic technique used to provide a feeling of depth is to make the foreground strong and the background weak (light). However, not everybody views a landscape in exactly the same way and so rather than allow himself to be tied down by rules, the artist should stress that part of the subject that interests him. Do not feel constrained by rules of perspective, rather draw the kind of picture you wish to produce, adding interest through contrast.

明度対比でムードをつくる
空の明度とほかを対比させ，2つの明度パターンに分けることで，遠近感を無視した絵づくりができる。

The contrast in lighting creates the mood of the picture.
By portraying the sky in a different brightness to the rest of the subject producing a contrast of two basic tones, you need not worry about perspective.

画面全体を明るい明度にすると，霧や雨で煙ったムードになる。このパターンに滲みを加えると効果的。

If the whole picture is done light, it gives the impression of rain or mist (this is even more effective if the Wet-in-Wet technique is used).

空を暗くして，ほかを明るくすると日差しの強い真昼のムードになる。

By coloring the sky dark and the rest of the picture light, it gives the impression of a bright noonday sun.

明度対比を左図と逆にすると，夕方か夜のムードになる。

If the contrast of tones is made the opposite of the picture on the left, it gives an impression of evening or night.

前景の建物を主役にする場合　The Buildings in the Foreground as Main Subject.

遠景の建物，空，道を暗くし，前景の建物は明るくして引き立てる。

The building in the background, the sky and the road should be made dark in order to make the front ones stand out.

左図と逆に主役の建物を暗く，ほかは明るくしてもよい。

However, it is equally acceptable to do the opposite and paint the main building dark and everything else light.

遠景の建物を主役にする場合　The Buildings in the Background as Main Subject.

主役になる建物を暗くし，ほかは明るくする。

The Buildings as main subject should be made dark in order to make everything else stand out.

左図と逆に主役を明るく，ほかを暗くしてもよい。

However, it is equally acceptable to do the opposite and paint the main subject light and everything else dark.

絵づくりのポイント

How To Produce a Picture

描き込みの度合い

Degrees of Detail

悪い例：前景の草を描き込み過ぎて，興味の中心となる中景の木立と後ろの山にいくべき焦点がボケてしまう。

A Bad Example : The grass in the foreground has been drawn in too much detail distracting the viewer's attention from the trees and mountain that are the main interest point of the picture.

良い例：前景の草は，興味の中心となる中景と描き込みのバランスを考えること。最初の明るい色だけにしておき，中景をある程度描き込んでから進めるとよい。透明水彩の場合，対象のすべてを描き込み過ぎると，まとまりのないバラバラな絵になってしまう。

A Good Example : Care was taken to balance the grass in the foreground with the main point of interest in the center of the picture. It is best if just the light color is painted first then the work done on the mid-distance before returning to the foreground. In the case of transparent watercolors, if too much detail is added, the picture becomes cluttered and does not mesh.

昼と夕方を明度で表す　Expressing Afternoon and Evening Through Contrast

昼：個々の対象を日なたと陰を明暗に分けて表す。遠景にいくにしたがい，大まかな明暗でとらえる。

Afternoon : The subject should be divided into sections of light and shade. As the subject moves into the distance, the contrast need only be expressed roughly.

早朝と夕方：空と水面を明るくして，ほかは細部を描き込まず，暗いシルエットとして表し，明度対比によるムードをつくる。

Dawn and Dusk : The sky and water should be light. None of the other details need be added, everything being depicted in silhouette and the mood evoked through contrast.

63

絵づくりのポイント

How To Produce a Picture

透明水彩の場合，果物の丸みの表現をするために，光と陰にこだわると，明暗の色の調和が難しくなるので，対象の形態，つまり曲面に沿った模様を描き込んだほうがうまくいく。

It is hard to express the roundness of fruit when using transparent watercolors as, if one concentrates on the light and shade, it becomes difficult to harmonize the colors. A better method is to use the brush strokes to follow the contours and depict the shape.

形態感を表す

Expressing Shape

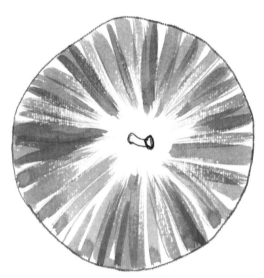

皿やテーブルに落ちる影のみをシンプルに描く。

Paint the shadow that falls on the plate or table very simply.

リンゴを真上から見ると芯を中心に 模様が放射状に広がっていることが分かる。

If the apple is looked at from above, it can be seen that the lines radiate out from the stem.

悪い例：模様が丸みに沿っていないと平面的なリンゴになる。

Bad Example : The lines do not follow the shape of the apple and it looks very flat.

良い例：模様はリンゴの丸みに沿って描くとリンゴの形態感が表現できる。

Good Example : When the strokes follow the contours of the apple, the shape is very well expressed.

リンゴの模様を曲面に沿ったタッチで描き，形態感を表す。

The pattern of the apple should be painted following the curve of the contours to express the shape.

ナシは曲面に沿ったタッチをドライブラシで描き，形態感を表す。

The curves of the Japanese pear should be expressed using a dry brush to depict the shape.

明快な模様のない場合，芯の部分を明るくぼかし，ナシの肌を滲みで変化をつけるだけでも感じはでる。

If there is no clear pattern, make the area around the stem light using a Gradated Wash. Use Wet-in-Wet when painting the skin of the Japanese pear to give it variation.

新緑の山を描く
Painting Spring Leaves on a Mountain

前景の新緑の繁み
New Leaves in the Foreground

1，黄緑を塗った上に緑を滲ませ，大まかな明暗をつける。

1. After painting the area in yellow-green, green should be blended in to give a rough feeling of light and dark.

2，乾かしてからさらに緑を塗り重ねる。

2. Once the paint has dried, build up with some more green.

3，乾かしてから，陰の緑を塗り重ねる。

3. After it has dried, build up with some dark green to produce shadows.

4，濡れているうちに水で湿らせた筆で色の境目を撫でてぼかし，下の色のとなじませる。

4. Use a wet brush to feather the edges of colors and make them merge with their neighbors.

中景の山
Central Mountains

スギは丸筆の穂先を揃え，タッチを生かす。

The cedars should be painted using the stroke of a round brush with the hairs brought together to a point.

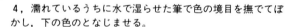

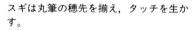

滲みを使って大まかな明暗をつける。

Use Wet-in-Wet to produce a rough shadowing.

さらにスギの木を滲ませる。境界のスギは滲みを使わず，はっきり表す。

Use Wet-in-Wet again to paint in the cedar trees. Do not use Wet-in-Wet for the trees on the skyline, these should be painted in clearly.

遠景の山
Distant Mountains

新緑を描くときは，混色して彩度を落とさず，絵具の色そのままのグリーンを使ったほうが新鮮でいきのよい色彩表現ができる。繁みも複雑な陰影をみせるが，葉を1枚1枚描くのではなく，単純化して，かたまりでとらえるとよい。細部にとらわれて，画面をいじりすぎると色が濁ってしまい，新緑の新鮮な雰囲気を損なってしまう。

手前の緑の山との対比が少し弱くなるが，基調色の青に緑を滲ませると，変化のあるおもしろい山が表現できる。

Although its contrast with the mountain in the foreground will be a little weak, use Wet-in-Wet to blend green into basic blue as this will provide an interesting effect.

When painting new leaves, the colors should not be mixed as that would make them lose their brightness, rather plain greens should be used to give a feeling of freshness. While the complicated shadows of the foliage should be shown, there is no need to express each leaf, it should be simplified and drawn as one object. If too much care is taken in fussing over each tiny detail, the colors will become muddy and the fresh feeling of the new leaves will be lost.

明度パターン
Brightness

遠景の山を暗くして，手前の新緑の明るさを引き立てる。

Keep the mountains in the background dark to make the foreground stand out.

樹木の繁みと幹
The Foliage and Trunks of Trees

悪い例：透明水彩の場合，幹や枝から描くと隠れるべき部分が繁みを透かして表れてしまう。

A Bad Example : When using transparent watercolors, if the trunk and branches are painted first, they will show through the lighter colors of the foliage.

良い例：樹木は繁みをのびのびとラフに彩色してから，幹や枝を丁寧に描くこと。

A Good Example : After the foliage of the tree was painted in roughly with lively stroke, the trunk and branches were painted in detail.

悪い例：繁みの緑に対し陰の色が暗すぎると，統一感が失われ全体がバラバラになってしまう。

A Bad Example : If the shadows are painted too dark in contrast to the green of the foliage, the picture will lose its unity.

良い例：明るい緑に対して陰も明るくして色のバランスを保つ。

A Good Example : The shadow in the light green foliage is also of light color, preserving the color balance.

繁みの陰は部分的に滲みを使い変化をつける。遠景の繁みは陰影をつけずフラットに塗る。

Use Wet-in-Wet for the foliage to produce variety. Do not add shading to the foliage in the distance, paint it flat.

悪い例：幹の色は赤みの強い茶色にしないこと。緑と赤は補色なのでどぎつい対比になる。

A Bad Example : A reddish-brown should not be used for the trunk of the tree as red and green are not complimentary colors and it produces a garish contrast.

良い例：幹の色は低彩度のグレーがかった色がよい。繁みの緑にちかい色で枝を描くと，葉を通して透けて見える感じがでる。

A Good Example : A greyish color is best for the trunk. If a color similar to that of the foliage is used for the branches it will create the impression that they are seen through the leaves.

針葉樹を描く
Painting Conifers

　針葉樹は，広葉樹に比べると形がはっきりしていて，明度も暗い。この両者を一緒に描くときは，明るい広葉樹から着手する。この場合，あまり形にこだわらずに，美しい滲みをつくることを心がけるとよい。完全に乾かしてから針葉樹を描く。このとき，手前にくる広葉樹の形も同時に整えることを忘れないようにする。

Compared to deciduous trees, conifers have a clearer shape and tend to be darker in color. When painting both kinds of tree together, start with the lighter deciduous. When doing this, do not spend too much time on detail, rather aim to have the colors blend. After the paint of the deciduous trees has completely dried, paint the conifers. When doing this, do not forget to tidy up the shape of the deciduous trees in the foreground.

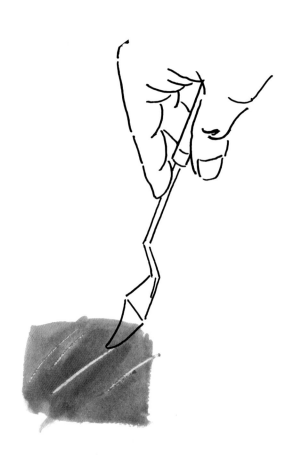

ススキ：ペインティングナイフの先で紙をひっかき，前景のススキの穂の白さを強める。

Grasses : Use the tip of a painting knife to scrape back the color and produce the white of the stems of the grass.

悪い例：描き込み過ぎると遠近のバラン
スをくずす。

A Bad Example : If too much detail is added the
feeling of depth is lost.

良い例：シルエットとして1色で表す。

A Good Example : A silhouette expressed in one color.

周囲の色を塗り，完全に乾かす。

Paint the surrounding color first and allow it to dry
completely.

木のシルエットを塗り重ねる。

Paint the silhouette of the trees on top.

わら屋根：穂先をバラバラにした筆で塗
り，わら屋根の材質感を表す。

Thatched Roofs : Splay the end of the brush to
produce a feeling of texture when painting thatch.

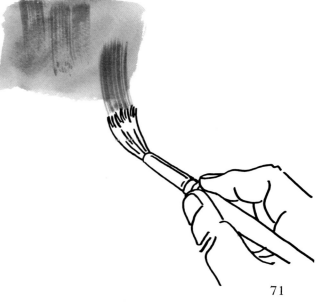

道を描く
Painting a Road

亀裂の描き方

How to Paint Cracks.

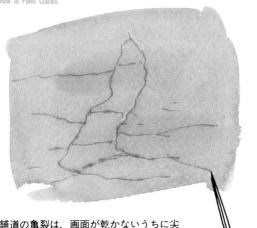

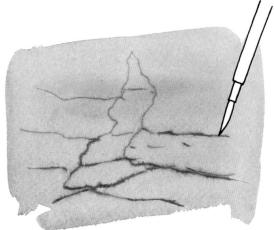

舗道の亀裂は，画面が乾かないうちに尖ったものでひっかくと，きずに絵具が染み込んでいく。

In order to depict the cracks in a surfaced road, use a pointed instrument to scratch the surface of the paint before it dries. The paint will soak into the scratches and produce the effect of cracks.

濃くしたい部分は面相筆で色を染み込ませ，乾かしてからドライブラシで左右にタッチをいれる。

To make dark patches let paint soak in using a features brush, then go over it again after it has dried with a dry brush to add brushstrokes to the edges.

運筆の悪い例：道の方向に沿って上下のタッチで描くのは間違い。

A Bad Example of Brush Technique : It is wrong to have the brush-strokes running down the road.

運筆の良い例：しっかりした道を描くには，筆を左右にのびのび運ぶこと。

A Good Example of Brush Technique : In order to present a realistic-looking road, the brush strokes should run smoothly across the road.

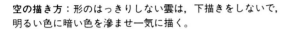

空の描き方：形のはっきりしない雲は，下描きをしないで，
明るい色に暗い色を滲ませ一気に描く。

How to Paint the Sky : In order to produce a hazy sky, it is not necessary to
sketch an outline first, just use the Wet-in-Wet technique to paint a dark
color over a light one.

草の描き方：材質感を表すときは，筆を
パレット上で押しつぶして，穂先をバラ
バラにしてタッチを描き入れる。目立ち
過ぎないように薄い色を使うとよい。

How to Paint the Grass : In order to bring out the
texture, splay the end of the brush by pressing it
against the palette before use. Use a light color
so it will not stand out too strongly.

雪山を描く
Painting a Snow-covered Mountain

　雪は用紙の白地をそのまま生かすので，周りのものとの明度対比が表現のポイントになる。そのため雪の陰影も，できるだけ明るく描き入れ，空や岩などと対比させて雪の白さを表すことになる。

The snow is depicted by the white of the paper so it is important to create a contrast with it and the surrounding areas. For this reason, the shadows in the snow should be painted as light as possible and the contrast with the sky or rocks used bring out the whiteness of the snow.

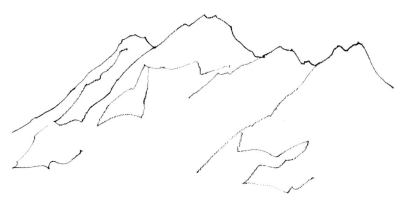

１，山の輪郭線と岩と雪の大きな境目が分かる程度に鉛筆で下描きをしておく。

1. Use a pencil to sketch the outline of the mountains and the division between the snow and the rocks.

２，岩を平塗りする。

2. Use a Flat Wash to color the rocks.

３，雪の陰を平塗りする。

3. Use a Flat Wash to fill in the shadows on the snow.

４，空を平塗りする。

4. Use a Flat Wash to fill in the sky.

雪は用紙の白を生かし，陰の色と岩の対比で表している。こ
のように色数の少ない雪景色は岩と雪の白いパターンの美し
さが生命なので，描き込みすぎてこわさないこと。

The snow uses the white of the paper, relying on the contrast with the
shadows and rocks to give it shape. With a subject like a snowscape with
very few colors, it is the pattern of the snow and rocks that brings it to life
so you must be careful not to spoil it by adding too much detail.

5，最後に岩の陰を塗り重ねる。

5. Finally build up the shadows of the rocks.

波紋と投影を描く
Painting Waves and Reflections

空の色を反映した水面　The Reflection of the Sky in the water.

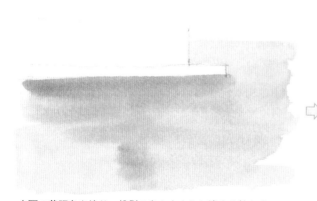

水面の基調色を塗り，投影の色を大まかに滲ませ乾かす。

Paint the basic color of the water then use the Wet-in-Wet technique to blend in the reflections.

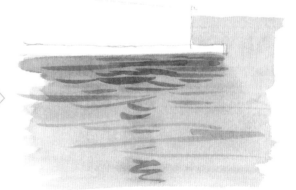

のびのびした水平のタッチを描きいれる。

Use long flowing strokes.

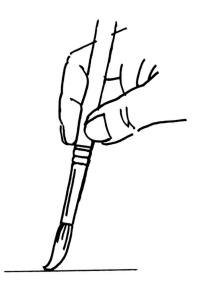

波紋の表現：筆を立て穂先を主に使い，長いのびのびしたタッチで描くとよい。

Expressing Waves : Hold the brush upright and just use the tip to create long, flowing strokes.

岸壁のテクスチャー

Texture of the Quay

水分を少なくした筆でスピーディに塗ると，かすれてザラついた材質感が得られる。

If you have little water on the brush and move it over the paper rapidly, the line will break up producing the texture of the stone.

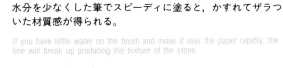

暖色，寒色をにじませ岸壁の基調色をつくる。

Use Wet-in-Wet to blend warm and cool colors to produce the base color of the quay.

穂の中程で塗る。

Use the middle of the brush to paint.

岩と波を描く
Painting Rocks and Waves

崖：大まかな陰影を滲ませてから，ザラついた感じをドライブラシで描き込む。

Cliff : Use Wet-in-Wet to roughly depict the shadows then use a dry brush to add the rough texture.

波がしらをかたまりでつかみ，陰影を滲ませる。

Think of the caps of the waves as a single object and use Wet-in-Wet to add the shadow.

白波以外の波のタッチも滲みをつかい，動きを表す。

Use Wet-in-Wet for the body of the wave too, in order to achieve a sense of movement.

コップを描く
How to Paint a Glass

悪い例：境界がデコボコしていてガラスのシャープな感じがない。

A Bad Example : The sharpness of the glass is missing.

良い例：境界をシャープにして，描き込む部分とあっさり描く部分の対比で表現する。

A Good Example : The outline is sharp and there is plenty of contrast between the areas that have been painted in detail and those that have only been done in rough.

悪い例：ハイライトや周りの写り込みを描き過ぎ。

A Bad Example : Too much care has been taken in painting the highlights and reflections of the surroundings.

良い例：滲みを使った内部のソフトな感じと境界のシャープなエッジとの対比で表現する。

A Good Example : Expressed by using Wet-in-Wet to create a soft feeling for the contents and contrasting it with the sharp edge of the glass.

陶器を描く
Painting China

下地を明るい色で塗る。ハイライトは紙の白地を生かす。

Paint the base with a light color. The white of the paper is used to express the highlights.

下地が乾かないうちに濃い色を重ねて滲ませる。

Before the base color has a chance to dry, add the dark color and allow it to blend.

暗くする部分は乾いてから塗り重ねる。

The dark areas should be built up after the paint has had a chance to dry.

ドライブラシ：筆に含ませた絵具を布に軽く押し当て，少し吸い取ってからスピーディに塗ると，うまくかすれる。

Dry Brush : Fill the brush with paint then soak up the excess on a piece of cloth. If the stroke is drawn rapidly, it will blur nicely.

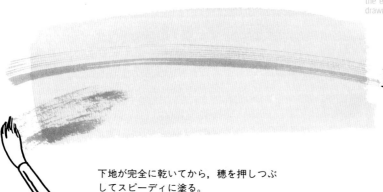

下地が完全に乾いてから，穂を押しつぶしてスピーディに塗る。

After the base paint has dried, splay the end of the brush and paint quickly.

堅い焼き物の肌の質感は，明暗の調子を大きなタッチであっさり描くとよい。

In order to achieve the hard feeling of the China, the light and dark tones should be applied with large strokes.

下地が完全に乾いてから模様を描く。模様は器のカーブに沿って1色で描くこと。

Apply the pattern after the base color has dried. The pattern should be painted in one color, following the curve of the object.

静物を描く
Painting Still Life

　形態に沿った線やタッチとぼかしの技法を併用して，丸みを表現してみよう。キノコやニンニクのように明るいものは，明暗をことさら強調しないで，淡いグレーであっさり調子をいれるのがコツ。タマネギは，滲みで描いたら明るい箇所をわずかにぼかし，形態にそった筋を描き入れるだけで，丸みは十分表現できる。作例のような題材は，陰影をつけすぎると，画面がうるさくなってまとまりを欠いてしまう。

The strokes should follow the shape of the object and be combined with a Gradated Wash to produce a feeling of roundness. Light objects such as mushrooms or garlic should not have heavy contrast and the shading is best applied using a light grey. The onion can be painted using Wet-in-Wet with a slight Gradated Wash used for the light area, lines can then be added to express the shape. With a subject such as this, if too much shadowing is applied, it will only make the picture seem cluttered and detract from its composition.

滲みとぼかしでさらっと描く。

Drawn simply with Wet-in-Wet and a Gradated Wash.

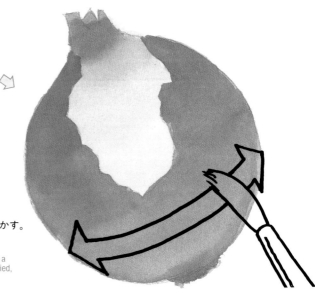

皮を平塗りしてから，水で湿らせた筆で左右に撫でてぼかす。乾かしてから丸みに沿った筋を描く。

After the skin has been colored using a Flat Wash, it is gradated using a brush with water on it and making horizontal strokes. Once this has dried, paint the veins following the contours of the shape.

陰影表現の基本

The Basic Technique of Expressing Shade and Shadow.

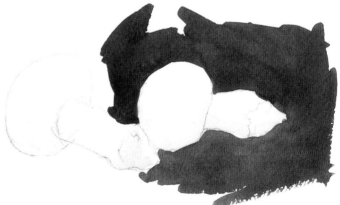

悪い例：陰が暗すぎる。上の明るい調子は描き込みすぎてうるさい。

A Bad Example： The shadow is too dark. If the light tone of the upper part is painted in too much detail, it becomes messy.

良い例：明るい対象の明暗の調子はこの程度を基本とする。また，バックを塗ることで仕上げるという考え方も必要。

A Good Example： With a light subject, this much shading is sufficient. One must remember that the background should be added before it can be considered finished.

ナスを描く
Painting an Eggplant

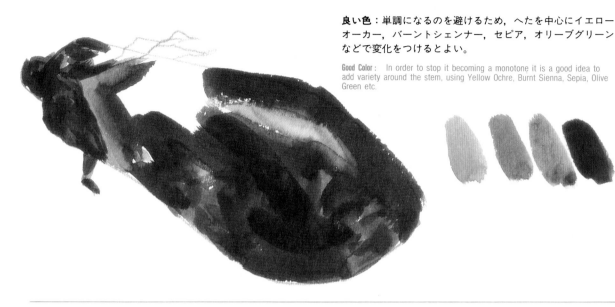

良い色：単調になるのを避けるため，へたを中心にイエローオーカー，バーントシェンナー，セピア，オリーブグリーンなどで変化をつけるとよい。

Good Color: In order to stop it becoming a monotone it is a good idea to add variety around the stem, using Yellow Ochre, Burnt Sienna, Sepia, Olive Green etc.

良い混色例 Example of a good color mix

プルッシアンブルー
Prussian Blue

＋

クリムソンレーキー
Crimson Lake

＝

彩度の高い暗いバイオレットがつくれる。ナスに限らず暗いバイオレットはこの混色でつくるとよい。

This produces a dark violet with a good color saturation. This is the best mix to produce a dark violet, not only for eggplants but any time it is needed.

ペイニーズグレー
Payne's Grey

＋

クリムソンレーキー
Crimson Lake

＝

プルッシアンブルーの場合より少し彩度の低いバイオレットになる。

This produces a violet with less color saturation than Prussian Blue.

プルッシアンブルー
Prussian Blue

＋

カドミウムレッドディープ
Cadmium Red Deep

＝

カドミウムレッドディープはクリムソンレーキーと比較してより彩度が低い色になる。

Cadmium Red Deep produces a color with less color saturation than Crimson Lake.

ペイニーズグレー
Payne's Gray

＋

カドミウムレッドディープ
Cadmium Red Deep

＝

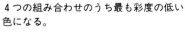

4つの組み合わせのうち最も彩度の低い色になる。

This color has the lowest color saturation of all four mixes.

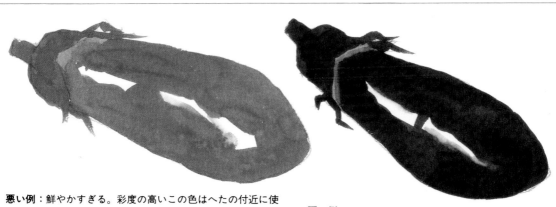

悪い例：鮮やかすぎる。彩度の高いこの色はへたの付近に使うとよい。

A Bad Example : Too bright. This color would be better used near the stem.

悪い例：明度は良いが単調。

Bad Example : The value is good but monotonous.

悪い混色例　An Example of a bad mix

バイオレット
Violet

イエロー
Yellow

イエローを加えて彩度を低くすると色味としては良くなるが、暗い色ができない。バイオレットをベースにするのは間違った混色である。

Adding yellow lowers the color saturation and produces a good hue, but it cannot be used when mixing a dark color. Using Violet as a base to mix the color is a mistake.

ブドウを描く
Painting Grapes

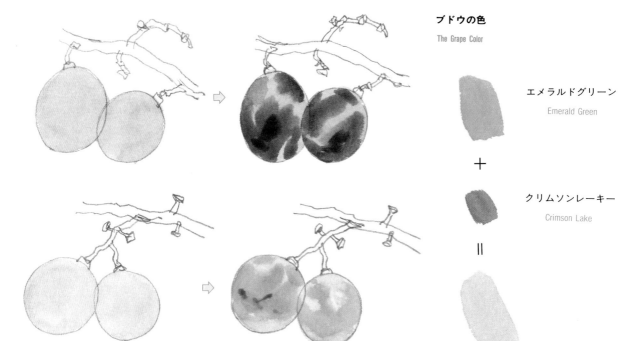

グレーを平塗りする。

Paint the grey as a Flat Wash.

白っぽい部分を残して基調色を滲ませ，乾いてから重ね塗りで加筆修正する。

Leaving whitish parts, blend in the base color using Wet-in-Wet.

ブドウの色
The Grape Color

エメラルドグリーン

Emerald Green

+

クリムソンレーキー

Crimson Lake

=

水の量を多くして絵具を薄く溶き，グリーンがかった明るいグレーをつくる。このグレーは果物の表面の粉がふいた感じを表す色として使う。

Use lots of water and dilute the paint to produce a bright green/grey. This grey is good for depicting the powder that forms on the fruit.

ブドウの陰影
Shading the Grapes

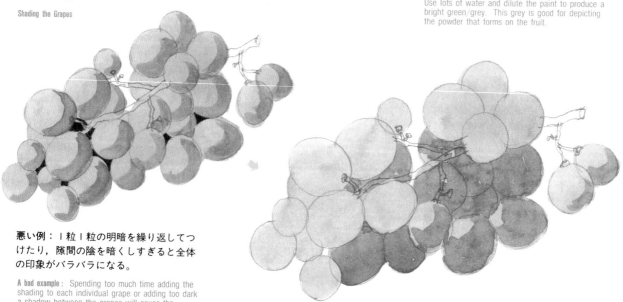

悪い例：1粒1粒の明暗を繰り返してつけたり，隙間の陰を暗くしすぎると全体の印象がバラバラになる。

A bad example: Spending too much time adding the shading to each individual grape or adding too dark a shadow between the grapes will cause the composition to fall apart.

良い例：全体を大きなかたまりとして明暗をとらえ，明るい基調色を全体に塗った上に陰の色を滲ませると，1房のブドウとしての一体感が表現できる。

A Good Example : The light and shade has been added as if to a single large object. By painting the light base color over the whole bunch and then blending in the shadow, it produces the effect of a bunch of grapes as a single unity.

マスカットのように明度が明るいものは，最初に思いっきり
明るい色を塗り，徐々に暗い色を重ねていくのがコツ。

With Muscat grapes which are a brighter color, first paint the light color
overall then build up using progressively darker paint.

巨峰は明度が暗く低彩度である。あまり派手なバイオレット
は使わず，バックになる皿を明るくして明暗を対比させるの
がコツ。

Black grapes nave a very dark tone so the trick is not to use too bright
violet but rather to place them in a light colored dish to create a good
contrast.

花を描く
Painting Flowers

水で湿らせた部分に基調色を塗り滲ませる。

Moisten the paper with water then use Wet-in-Wet to add the base color.

斑点を滲ませる。下の色が乾いたら水で湿らせてから塗るとよい。

Blend in the spots, if the bottom color has dried, moisten it again with water.

明るいピンク，暗いピンクの順に滲ませる。シベは最後に不透明水彩（ガッシュ）で描き起こす。

Use Wet-in-Wet to add the light pink then the dark pink. Add the stamen last, using opaque watercolor (gouache).

イエロー，明るいグリーンを塗る。

Apply Yellow and Bright Green.

葉，茎は1色で白い花の部分も塗りつぶす。

Paint the stem and leaves in one color, covering the area of the white flower.

不透明水彩で白い花，茎の明るい部分を描き起こす。

Then add the flower and highlights in the stem using white opaque watercolor.

ぼかしの方法

Gradation Technique

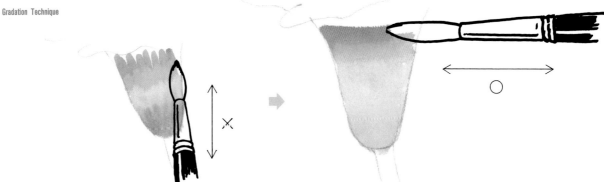

悪い例：上下にぼかすときは筆を縦に動かすと失敗する。

A Bad Example : When gradating from top to bottom, the brush should not be moved vertically.

良い例：筆を左右に動かしてぼかしたほうが効果的。

A Good Example : A much better effect is achieved if the brush is moved horizontally.

バラを描く
Painting a Rose

　バラに限らず花を題材にするときは，絵の主役を際立たせるため，花そのものをていねいに，葉や茎はラフに描くとよい。バラの場合，複雑に重なり合っている花弁を下描きの段階で，線をしっかりとらえることが大切になる。

When using any flower as the subject of a picture one should paint the flower in detail but only fill in the leaves and stems roughly, this has the effect of making the main subject stand out. In the case of a rose, it is important to grasp the line of the complicated pattern of petals when drawing the rough sketch.

花の描き方 How to Draw a Flower

1，花弁の形は丁寧に下描きする。

1. Draw in the shape of the petals carefully.

2，花の基調色を全体に塗る。

2. Paint the whole flower in the base color.

3，対象に異なった色があったら滲ませる。この段階までは全体を平面でとらえ、個々の花弁の区別をしていない。

3. If there are petals of different colors, allow them to blend. At this stage grasp the shape as a whole and don't worry about the individual petals.

4，完全に乾いてから個々の陰を描き立体感をつける。

4. After the paint has completely dried, apply shadows to each flower and create a feeling of depth.

葉の描き方　How to paint the leaves

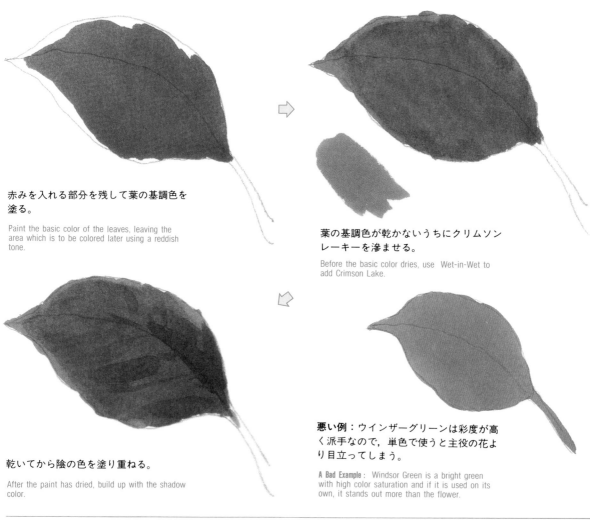

赤みを入れる部分を残して葉の基調色を
塗る。

Paint the basic color of the leaves, leaving the
area which is to be colored later using a reddish
tone.

葉の基調色が乾かないうちにクリムソン
レーキーを滲ませる。

Before the basic color dries, use Wet-in-Wet to
add Crimson Lake.

乾いてから陰の色を塗り重ねる。

After the paint has dried, build up with the shadow
color.

悪い例：ウインザーグリーンは彩度が高
く派手なので，単色で使うと主役の花よ
り目立ってしまう。

A Bad Example : Windsor Green is a bright green
with high color saturation and if it is used on its
own, it stands out more than the flower.

葉の色
The leaf color

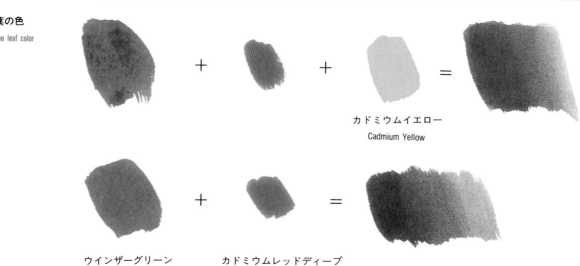

カドミウムイエロー
Cadmium Yellow

ウインザーグリーン
Windsor Green

カドミウムレッドディープ
Cadmium Red Deep

"がく" の描き方　How to paint the Calyx

明るいグリーンを塗る。

Paint a light green.

先端に赤みをつけるため，クリムソンレーキーを滲ませる。

Add red to the tip using Crimson Lake.

明るい花の場合

In the case of a light-colored flower

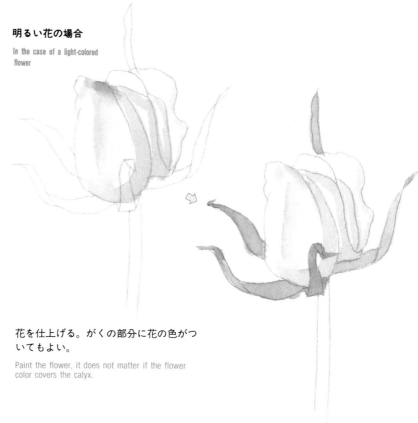

花を仕上げる。がくの部分に花の色がついてもよい。

Paint the flower, it does not matter if the flower color covers the calyx.

がくを描く。白に近い色の場合，がくを重ねても発色に影響ない。

Paint the calyx. With a nearly white flower, it will make no difference to the color if the calyx lies over the flower.

暗い花の場合　In the case of a dark Flower

花と重なっているがくから描く。

Start painting with the calyx that lie over the petals.

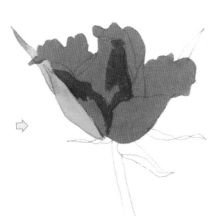

花は，がくに食い込まないように丁寧に描く。

Paint in the petals taking care not to cover the calyx.

外のがくは花弁を仕上げてから描く。

The outer calyx can be painted after the petals have been completed.

描く手順　Painting Order

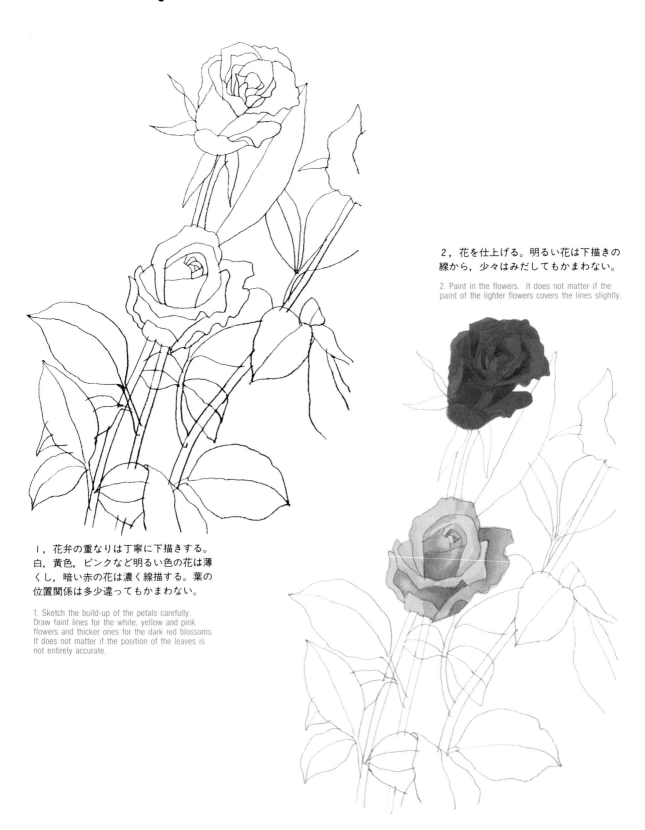

２，花を仕上げる。明るい花は下描きの
線から，少々はみだしてもかまわない。

2. Paint in the flowers. It does not matter if the
paint of the lighter flowers covers the lines slightly.

１，花弁の重なりは丁寧に下描きする。
白，黄色，ピンクなど明るい色の花は薄
くし，暗い赤の花は濃く線描する。葉の
位置関係は多少違ってもかまわない。

1. Sketch the build-up of the petals carefully.
Draw faint lines for the white, yellow and pink
flowers and thicker ones for the dark red blossoms.
It does not matter if the position of the leaves is
not entirely accurate.

4，茎，葉の陰をつける。明るい葉は手前，暗い葉は後ろとして前後感を表す。

4. Add shadow to the stem and leaves. The brighter leaves fall in the front and the darker ones to the rear, giving depth to the picture.

3，重なり合う箇所があるので，それぞれ乾いてから色を塗る。がく，茎，葉の順で彩色する。

3. There are some sections where the objects overlap and these should be added after the paint has dried. The calyx should be colored first, then the stem then the leaves.

人形を描く
Painting Dolls

そばに置いてじっくり観察できる人形は，様式化され人間とは異なるが，髪や衣装の彩色に関しては，人物を描くための参考になる題材でもある。

A doll is not a person, but as it can be placed in a convenient position and studied carefully it is useful for practicing the coloring of the clothes and hair and is a useful reference for painting people.

髪の描き方

Painting the Hair

悪い例：陰影を細かく描くと強いアクセントが全体に散らばって，まとまりを欠いてしまう。

A Bad Example : If the shading is too broken up it becomes a strong accent and tends to detract from the unity of the picture.

良い例：目を細めて大きな明暗をつけるとよい。

A Good Example : Half close the eyes and just pick up the main area of light and dark.

顔の描き方

How to paint the face

悪い例：陰の色が暗過ぎるし，明暗の調子も光の方向性がないため単調。

A Bad Example : The shadow is too dark and the contrast of the shading does not indicate the direction of the light making the result monotonous.

良い例：右上からの光でできる陰を明るめにつける。顔の調子をつけ過ぎて説明過剰にしないこと。

A Good Example : The shading for a light from the top right is added lightly. Do not over-express the tone of the face.

衣服の調子

The Tone of the clothes

悪い例：しわの陰を全部同じ調子で描くと，まとまりがない絵になってしまう。

A Bad Example : If all the shadows on the clothes are painted in the same tone the picture will not come together.

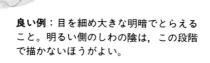

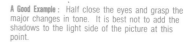

良い例：目を細め大きな明暗でとらえること。明るい側のしわの陰は，この段階で描かないほうがよい。

A Good Example : Half close the eyes and grasp the major changes in tone. It is best not to add the shadows to the light side of the picture at this point.

顔を描く
Painting The Face

顔を描くときは，目の大きさはどうか，鼻の長さ，唇の形はどうなっているか，鼻の幅と比較して大きいか，小さいかをチェックポイントにして観察することだ。モデルに似る，似ないは各部分の形と長さ，幅，位置関係の比較で決まる。

When painting the face the points to watch for when viewing the subject are : the size of the eyes, the length of the nose, the shape of the lips and the width of the nose. Whether the finished picture will resemble the model or not depends on the shape, length, width and relative position of the various features.

顔の制作手順 The Order When Painting a Face

肌の色を頭部まで塗るのは，額にかかる髪の形を後で塗り重ねるためである。

The flesh tone is painted to the top of the head as the hairstyle will be painted over it later.

陰の色を塗り重ねる。

The shadows are added using the Overpainting.

乾かしてからさらに中間の調子を重ねる。顔は3段階の色の調子で描くことになる。

After the paint has dried, add the mid-tone shading. The face is painted in three stages.

悪い例：肌の色を塗るときは，頭髪の色，唇の色をはっきり分けない。

A Bad Example : When painting the skin tone, there is no clear difference between the areas of hair color and lip color.

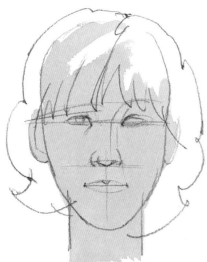

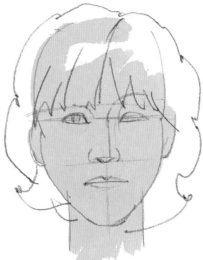

イエローオーカーをベースにして，カドミウムレッドの量を加減する。

Use Yellow Ochre as a base and add Cadmium Red sparingly.

彩度を低くした肌色をつくるときは，セルリアンブルーを少量混ぜるとよい。

In order to mix a skin tone with a low color saturation, add a small amount of Cerulean Blue.

カドミウムレッドの量を多くすると，赤みがかった肌色ができる。

If too much Cadmium Red is used, the skin tone will become reddish.

混色でつくる肌色：水で薄めて明るくすることが基本。

Skin-tone, made by mixing paints :　Add water to lighten it.

 + = 　　 + =

イエローオーカー	カドミウムレッド	日本人の肌色の基準色	カドミウムレッド	イエローオーカー	赤味がかった肌色
Yellow Ochre	Cadmium Red	The basic skin tone for Japanese.	Cadmium Red	Yellow Ochre	A reddish skin tone

 + + =　　 + + =

イエローオーカー	カドミウムレッド	セルリアンブルー	低彩度の肌色	イエローオーカー	カドミウムレッド	セルリアンブルー	肌の陰の色
Yellow Ochre	Cadmium Red	Cerulean Blue	A skin tone with a low color saturation.	Yellow Ochre	Cadmium Red	Cerulean Blue	Shadow on skin tone.

肌の色

全体の色の調和を図るため，衣服の色や
バックの色との関係で，肌に固有色以外
の色味を入れることも必要になる。

The skin tone
In order to harmonize the skin tone with the
subject's clothes or background, it is necessary to
add reflected color to the skin tone.

固有色以外の色味は明るい色を少し滲ま
せる。

Add the reflected color using Wet-in-Wet to blend
in light tones.

肌の明るい色を平塗りしてから赤，青を
滲ませる。

After adding the skin tone as a Flat Wash, use
Wet-in-Wet to add red and blue.

乾かしてから，肌の陰の色を重ね塗りす
る。

After the paint has dried, Overpaint to add the
shadows

目の描き方

Painting the Eyes

１，鉛筆の下描き。

1. Sketch with pencil.

２，うわまぶたが落とす影を目の丸みに
沿って，薄いグレーで塗る。

2. Fill in the shadow of the upper eyelid on the
eye with a light grey.

３，黒目を塗る。

3. Paint the iris.

４，円に沿って薄い調子をつけたら，真
ん中の黒い瞳を塗る。

4. Add light tone around pupil then paint in the
black pupil.

５，ハイライトをホワイトで入れる。

5. Use white to add highlights.

髪の描き方　How to Paint the Hair

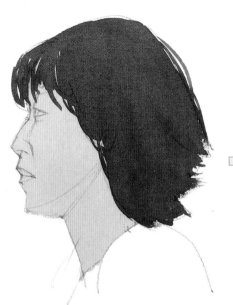

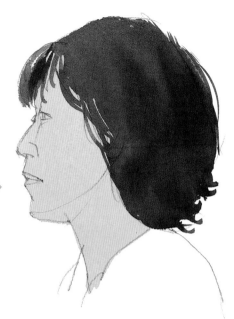

最終的に残す明るい色を平塗りする。顔
との境目は慎重に塗ること。

Paint the lightest color in the hair as a Flat Wash,
taking care not to cross the border with the face.

暗い色を滲ませる。この程度で完成とし
ても十分。

Blend in the darker color using Wet-in-Wet. It is
quite acceptable to consider the hair finished at
this point.

乾かしてから，滲ませた色をあっさり重
ねる程度でよい。

Once the paint has dried, build up the darker color.

髪は外側の形が決め手になるので，内側
はあまり細かく描き込まないこと。

The hair is decided by the shape of the outer part,
do not bother to add too much detail to the center.

悪い例：頭髪を１本１本描くと，髪の質
感のみ際立って他とのバランスがとれな
い。

A Bad Example：If the hair is painted in strand by
strand, it will stand out too much and will not
balance with the rest of the picture.

衣服の模様
The Pattern on Clothes

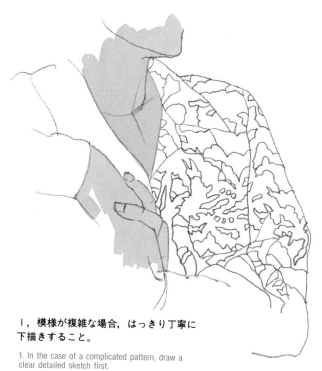

１，模様が複雑な場合，はっきり丁寧に
下描きすること。

1. In the case of a complicated pattern, draw a
clear detailed sketch first.

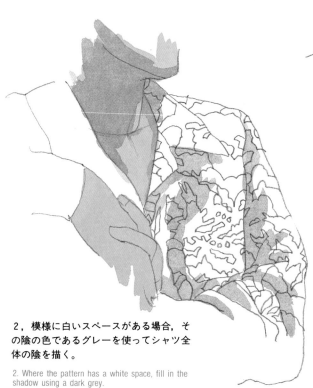

２，模様に白いスペースがある場合，そ
の陰の色であるグレーを使ってシャツ全
体の陰を描く。

2. Where the pattern has a white space, fill in the
shadow using a dark grey.

３，それぞれの固有色を平塗りで重ねる
と，明暗の２段階の模様が表現できる。

3. Add each of the colors, using a Flat Wash, you
can express the patterns in two levels of light and
dark.

1，明るい模様から先に描くこと。

1. Paint the light pattern first.

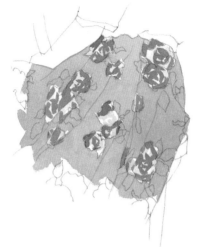

2，模様に重ならないようにスカートの明るい地色を塗る。

2. Paint the light base color of the skirt, ensuring it does not overlap.

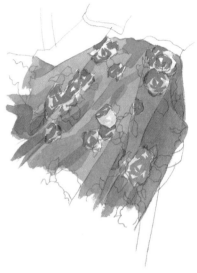

3，さらに地の陰の色を重ねる。

3. Add the shadows of the base color using Overpainting.

4，明るい模様が陰になる部分は同系色で暗い色をつくって重ねる。最後に暗い模様を地の色に塗り重ねる。

4. Mix the paint for the shadow on the light pattern using a darker tone of the same color. Finally add the dark pattern, painting over the base color.

水溶性の色鉛筆とクレヨンを併用。部分的にタッチを残すと
効果的。

If you use water soluble pencils and crayons in unison with watercolor
paints, you will find them very useful for adding small areas of detail.

色鉛筆（水溶性）でスケッチする。

Draw a sketch using colored pencils (water soluble).

水を含ませた筆で画面を撫で，色を溶かす。水は，少なめに
含ませたほうがよい。

Go over the area with a wet brush lightly feathering the lines, causing them
to dissolve.
It is best if the brush does not have too much water on it when doing this.

水溶性の色鉛筆とクレヨン

　線や調子をつけてスケッチした後，水を含ませた筆で撫でると，色が溶けて水彩と同じような効果のでる色鉛筆は，色数が豊富に揃っていて，芯も細くかなり描き込みができる便利な画材だ。スケッチにとどまらず，色鉛筆と水彩を併用したイラストレーションに使うと，おもしろい効果が期待できる。同様の性質をもつクレヨンタイプは，太く描けるので，ラフなスケッチに便利。

水溶性の色鉛筆とクレヨン
Water Soluble Colored Pencils and Crayons.

Water Soluble Colored Pencils and Crayons.

After drawing the rough sketch using a water soluble colored pencil, go over the lines with a wet brush and the color will run in just the same way as watercolor paints. Colored pencils come in a variety of colors and they can be used for fine detail making them a useful tool. You need not stop with just a sketch, but use both colored pencils and watercolors in unison to create an interesting effect. The crayons have the same ability to dissolve in water but they produce much thicker lines and are ideal to use when drawing a rough sketch.

水溶性のクレヨンは太い線で描ける。
水で溶かすときタッチを少し残すと効果的。

The water soluble crayons produce thickerlines. It is effective to remain the touch of brush when dissolving in water.

用具の後始末

　透明水彩の用具は水で処理できるので簡単だが，描いたあとは，きれいに洗っておかないと絵具がこびりついて取れなくなってしまう。とくにピンクやバイオレットはこの傾向があるので注意。また，パレットに詰めた絵具の補充を忘れないようにしよう。固めた絵具が凹凸に減っていると筆を傷めるので，平らに詰めること。なお，絵具に含まれている溶剤が湿気で溶け出し，表面に透明な膜をつくることがある。これが固まると絵具が使えなくなるので，早いうちに水を含ませた筆で取ることも必要になる。

Caring For One's Equipment

Transparent watercolor paints are soluble in water so they are very convenient, but care must be taken to clean the equipment after use or the paint will dry on it and become impossible to remove. Pink and Violet are particularly prone to do this so care should be taken when using these colors. Care should also be taken to see that the paint on the palette is not running low. If deep depressions have been worn in the paints, it will harm the brushes so they should be refilled to produce a smooth, flat surface. Sometimes the solvent in the paint will melt and come to the top of the paint, forming a transparent coating. If this is allowed to harden the paint will become unusable so it should be cleaned off with a wet brush as soon as possible.

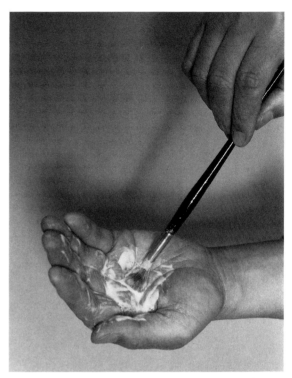

筆の手入れ：きれいな水で洗い，布でふきとり穂先を揃えておくだけで十分。穂の根元の絵具は落ちにくいので，ときどきは，石鹸で洗うようにしよう。

Caring for Brushes: It is sufficient if the brushes are washed in water, dried on a cloth and the hairs smoothed into position. Sometimes paint will build up at the base of the hairs and if this happens it should be washed off with soap.

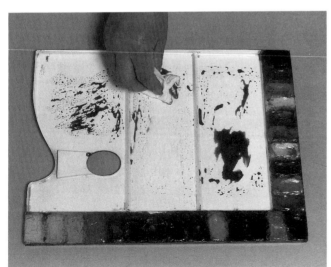

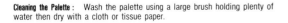

パレットの掃除：大きな筆に水を含ませて，絵具を洗い流し，布かティッシュペーパーでふきとる。

Cleaning the Palette: Wash the palette using a large brush holding plenty of water then dry with a cloth or tissue paper.

水彩用紙

　水彩紙1枚の全紙サイズは，メーカーによって多少異なるが，76×57センチ位を目安にするとよい。これを好みのサイズに裁断するにはカッターでもよいが，用紙の縁が鋭くなるので，手を切る恐れがある。写真のように床において金属の定規を当て，足でしっかり固定して端から破るように引っ張る簡単な方法もある。この方法だと縁がギザギザになって，デックレッジ（耳つき）のように見映えよく，縁もソフトで安全に使える。

Paper for Watercolor Painting

The size of paper for watercolor painting varies slightly according to the manufacturer but on average it is about 76 cm. by 57 cm. The paper can be cut to a suitable size using a cutter, but the edge of the paper will be very sharp and care must be taken not to cut one's hands. A better method is to hold the paper down on the floor and tear it along a straight edge. This will produce a rough edge that is both attractive and safe.

ウォーターマーク：水彩用紙を透かして見てメーカーのマークが読み取れる側が表面。

Watermark: Hold the paper up to the light and look at the watermark. The side that shows the watermark the right way around is the front.

アルシュ紙のウォーターマーク

The watermark in Arches paper.

水張りの方法

　水彩用紙は，41ページの制作手順のように，マスキングテープで4辺を画板にとめるだけでも，彩色にはさしつかえない。厚手の用紙はあまり問題ないが，薄手の用紙の場合，制作中に画面が波打って描きにくくなるのを嫌う人は，本格的に水張りをしたものを使うと，気持ちよく描ける。紙は水に濡れると伸び，乾くと収縮するという原理を応用した以外に簡単な方法なので，試してみよう。

Stretching Paper

As mentioned on page 41, the paper need only be fastened to a drawing board with tape on each of its four sides before it can be used for painting, but while this is adequate for thick paper, thin paper tends to wrinkle when it is wet and some people find it difficult to use. In order to avoid this problem the paper can be stretched, a simple process that makes use of the fact that paper stretches when wet and shrinks again when it dries. The steps involved in this are quite easy and are as follows.

水張りの材料と用具：パネル，刷毛，カッターナイフ，水張り用テープ，水彩用紙

Materials required for stretching paper : Board, paste brush, cutter/knife, special adhesive tape, paper.

１，用紙は，パネルより周囲１センチ大きく切る。

1. Cut the paper so it is larger than the board by about one centimeter in each direction.

２，用紙の裏面に刷毛で水をたっぷりとまんべんなくつけ，15分位放置しておく。

2. Coat the rear of the paper evenly with water using the brush. Pick up the paper and allow the excess water to drain.

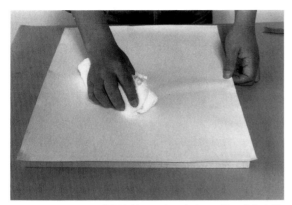

３，パネルにのせ，表面を乾いた布で中心から縁へ空気を追い出すように押して密着する。

3. Place the paper on the board upright and using a piece of cloth, brush out from the center to remove all the air.

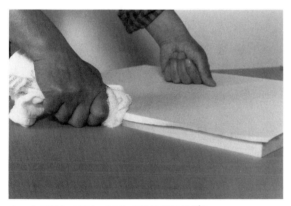

４，布で押し４辺をパネルの縁に折り曲げる。

4. Press down with the cloth on the edges of the board to crease the paper.

５，角を折り曲げ，セロハンテープで仮留めする。

5. Fold down the edges of the paper and fasten it temporarily with scotch tape.

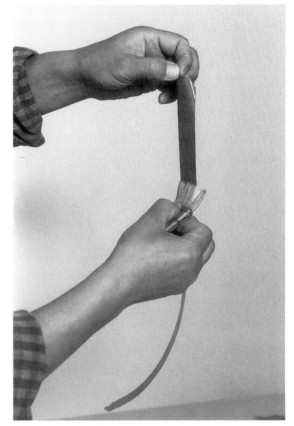

６，水張り用テープを４辺の長さに合わせて切り，刷毛で水をつける。

6. Cut four lengths of the adhesive tape to match the size of the board and wet the glue with the brush.

７，折り曲げた４辺の上を５ミリ位残し，テープを張りつける。表面が波打っていても，乾くときれいに平らになる。

7. Leaving approximately 5 mm. from the edge of the board, fasten the four sides down with the tape. It does not matter if the surface is not quite smooth as it will shrink as it dries to produce a perfect surface.

おわりに
Afterword

　本書は，アマチュアを指導することに20年以上たずさわっ
ている筆者の経験を生かし，これから透明水彩を始めようと
する人や，描いても一向にうまくならないという人のために
透明水彩の基本的な技法を解説したものです。
　なにごとによらず基本というのは，あまりおもしろいもの
ではありません。しかし，透明水彩の良さも難しさも，基本
的な画材の知識や平塗り，滲み，ぼかしの技法を抜きにして
語れません。基本をマスターしたら，自由にそして大胆に描
く，迷ったら基本に戻る。この繰り返しが，透明水彩を自分
のものにする一番よい方法だと思います。

In writing this book, the author has been able to call on over
twenty years' experience in teaching amateurs. All the basic
techniques used in painting with transparent watercolors are
covered and it is aimed at beginners or those who find that
they are unable to improve their technique.
While nobody likes to concentrate solely on the basic
techniques, the best and most difficult part of watercolors
lies in such basics as a knowledge of the materials used, Flat
Wash, Wet-in-Wet and Gradated Washes. Once these basics
have been mastered, one can begin to develop one's own
style, but should the need arise, the basic techniques are
always there to fall back upon. In this way, one can learn
in easy stages and eventually master the medium of
transparent watercolors.

松原　龍夫
TATSUO MATSUBARA
1941年富山県生まれ。
現代日本美術展，ジャパンアートフェスティバル，ビエ
ラ国際版画ビエンナーレなどに出品多数，個展を中心に
作家活動を行っている。現在，講談社フェーマススクー
ルズインストラクター，NHK 文化センター，東急クリエ
イティブライフ・BE 講師。

The Author : Tatsuo Matsubara
Born Toyama Prefecture, 1941
Concentrating on private exhibitions he also exhibited in
the 'Exhibition of Contemporary Japanese Art' and the '
Liberian International Print Biennale.' At present he
teaches at the Kodansha Famous Schools and the NHK
Culture Center.

透明水彩で描く

1991年 3 月25日　初版第 1 刷発行
1993年 9 月25日　初版第 6 刷発行
1994年 6 月25日　初版第 7 刷発行
1995年12月15日　初版第 8 刷発行

著　　　者　　松原龍夫ⓒ
発 行 者　　久世利郎
印刷製本　　日本写真印刷株式会社
写　　植　　三和写真工芸株式会社
発 行 所　　株式会社グラフィック社
　　　　　　〒102 東京都千代田区九段北1-9-12
　　　　　　☎03(3263)4318 Fax.03(3263)5297
　　　　　　振替・00130-6-114345
　　　　　　ISBN4-7661-0622-9 C2371